PATH TO SALES

EXPLORING SALES ONE STEP AT A TIME

ERIK WILT

This book is dedicated to my father,
William John Wilt.

Dad, even though you will never thumb through these pages,
each page emits your incredible influence on my life.
I miss you and love you.

ACKNOWLEDGEMENTS

Julio Hernandez and Shelly Smith, I thank you for your care and coaching. Jonathan Frost, you're my brother and kindred spirit. Gina and Dru Kiesel, thank you for your tireless support. Angie Marthaller and Eric Bernier thank you for your partnership and companionship as habit pioneers. Mom and Stacey, thank you for always being there and never giving up on me. Thank you, Carrie, and Tom Smith for giving me the love of my life. Abigail, Ella, Jonathan and Matthew thank you for changing my world in amazing ways on a daily basis. Linsey, there are no words that can express how much you mean to me... I love you.

CONTENTS

INTRODUCTION:

Trailhead

THERE'S NO SHORTAGE OF BOOKS on sales available. Typing "sales" into Amazon yields nearly 900,000 results. There are books written from every imaginable perspective. They're written by leaders in sales, traditional sales gurus, "outsiders" with disruptive ideas, and even those who claim to have the "secret" to sales. Each person who leaves his or her mark on the world of sales by writing a book on the topic does so with every intention of being creative and unique. So you might ask yourself, "Do we really need *another* book on sales?" I am here to tell you that in fact, we do.

Each perspective on sales is unique, different, and important. As each author communicates his or her nuggets of information, we learn profound truths. There are many different paths available to get to the same destination; these books cover all of them, thereby making it possible for so many different personalities to succeed in a sales career. And yet every book contains flaws based on assumptions, providing the next writer with an opportunity to make improvements.

For the rookie and veteran alike, a good book on sales will do the same thing: it will inspire. That's another reason there are so many sales books available today. Every day, salespeople set out on an uphill battle where they face hard work and potential rejection. Cracking a book open in the middle of a difficult day might mean the difference between closing a big sale or handing in a resignation letter. Most of the professional salespeople I know morphed into avid readers over time just to keep from quitting the game. They would read book after book and draw from the principles and stories at just the right time. With each page they would receive timely encouragement along with hints on how they could up their game. Book after book, they begin to set themselves apart and find themselves reaching the summit with the other top producers.

From an early age I was a passionate reader. I believe that reading was an important factor in leading me to sales. After I finished each book I would summarize it to anyone who would listen. I was especially rewarded when a friend or colleague picked up the book I was promoting to read for him or herself. As a teen, I spent a lot of time reading and sharing stories from the King James Bible. As well known as the Bible is, I found it to be a pretty tough sell to a lot of people. In those early high school years, I attended Bible studies, which I eventually came to think of as biblical sales talks. I wasn't aware at the time, but this ecclesiastical part of my journey was helping to shape a successful future in sales and communication. To this day, I refer to the church as the largest sales force in the world.

The stage of the church primed my appetite for sales like nothing else I'd experienced. Through my experience as a church youth leader and pastor, I was asked to speak to groups of people, serve without pay, show up to meetings when I didn't feel like it, and focus on cost and value. By working as part of team responsible for launching new churches, I was thrust into positions of leadership and management, and I learned all the things it takes to build a successful business from the ground up. Relationship after relationship and book after book, my sales acumen grew along with my experience in ministry. At first, I was conflicted when I saw the connection between sales and religion. My father had raised me to be cautious of salespeople because that's what he was. He had experienced commission-hungry schemers and wanted to protect me from what he had experienced. Over the years, I came to understand that there is good and bad to be found in church and sales because the common thread is humanity. That's something no father can protect a son from.

My dad started to dismantle his warnings around a sales career in the years that followed. Immediately following our wedding, my wife and I moved to upstate New York to be part of a team launching a new church. Because of the distance, my dad and I would talk on the phone multiple times a week. He would tell me tales of the family drama happening on the West Coast and I would moan over the culture shock we were feeling in the Northeast. In those phone calls I learned that my dad actually loved sales because he loved helping people. We started to relate to one another in our desire to help people solve problems, him in sales and me through the church. We found that we weren't so different and I found myself wanting to be like my salesman dad instead of a church pastor. I had no idea at the time that my career path would eventually merge with his.

Sales would rear its head again as we pursued the American dream of business ownership. With no college degree and a strong back I worked construction to put food on the table while building a coffee shop business at night with my wife and in-laws. The business became a hit in the community and did well, but our rise was cut short by eminent domain. After all the blood, sweat, and tears we put into establishing a local drive-through coffee kiosk that the community loved, we had to pack up and make way for a road that is rarely traveled. The heartbreak of having to close our doors didn't defeat us; it fueled our desire to work harder. The customer relationships and stories we have from that time could fill a book, but the lesson we learned was that we were addicted to the American dream.

Later we moved to Virginia, where another coffee shop attempt fizzled out in failure. There were also network marketing opportunities that never panned out. Each book we read gave us additional motivation to keep pushing, but at what cost? We began to feel like we were trapped in our own version of the Bill Murray movie *Groundhog Day*, repeating the same day over and over. It seemed like each failure we endured was telling us to give up on the dream of business ownership, wake up, and find some real-world jobs.

With the debt from our failed business attempts paid off, we decided to make a change. My leadership experience paved the way for me to accept a very good day job working as a project supervisor and superintendent on a very large construction project in Denver, Colorado. We moved again and I decided to give up on that elusive American dream and keep my head down and work hard. But that was easier said than done; I couldn't keep myself from reading and learning, so the dream never truly died.

If I couldn't force my way into business, I figured I could learn what I was doing wrong, so to do that, I started working toward a business degree. I learned a lot of great stuff but nothing compared to what I learned in the books I was reading on the side. As part of my college curriculum I would read books by deep-thinking professors expounding on important business principles. But I realized what these professors lacked was field experience; they'd spent their time in classrooms, not in the field. I valued my experience as a college student, but I credit my success in sales and business to mildly educated salespeople writing books that I read in my spare time.

Soon after that I started a cabin-building business and for the first time I broke even. I was building cabins, and things were starting to make sense. I was engaging with people and my business was growing. I learned that building cabins is back-breaking work and I realized I was starting to love the sales side of business. Coming to terms with what cabin building was doing to my body, I finally admitted to myself that I just might be cut out for a career in sales after all. Many of my friends who worked in skilled trades wanted to work with their hands, but I was finding that I would rather work with people. Learning that I could make a better life for my family without breaking my back strengthened my resolve to make the change.

After accepting my first job selling insurance, I realized that I had been unintentionally honing my sales acumen for years. I started setting rookie sales records in my office, achieved rookie of the year status, and was consistently ranked in the top five producers in the region. Management offers were quick to come and the majority of office training and development became my responsibility. I continued to rank in the top 5% while splitting most of my commissions with the rookies I was training. Sales success had snuck up on me through the books I'd been reading.

It was the simple things that made a difference. Principles from Dale Carnegie's *How to Win Friends and Influence People* taught me how to engage with colleagues and clients. John C. Maxwell illustrated personal change in *Winning with People,* and I learned powerful self-management from Rory Vaden in *Procrastinate on Purpose.* Looking back at my collection of books is like looking at the stepping-stones to my success in sales. In retrospect, I became a product of what I was reading in those books so success became inevitable.

Reading books is time consuming. We all have limited time, so I thought it would be great to consolidate the information I learned. I looked for a book that combined many of the elements I was learning from proprietary training but I never found it. I would see effective techniques being used across different industries, yet I couldn't find a book that consolidated these common sales principles in one place. I also wanted a book that would be fun to read. I wanted stories and personalities, not just facts, figures, and philosophies. I wanted a book that would appeal to the professional salesperson, novice, or someone pondering a career in sales.

Successful people initiating the change they seek is a reoccurring theme in every great business and personal development book I've ever read. After searching for years without finding what I wanted, I decided to be the change I was looking for. The result of this quest is the book you now hold in your hands. I wrote it to fill a void on my bookshelf and I hope you'll find it useful as well.

I don't expect this book to replace others on sales, personal development, or business. Rather, the goal of this book is to enhance what you have access to by adding perspective. I learned a long time ago that it's not what you say but how you say it. It is my sincere hope that this book sharpens truths you might already know or reminds you about forgotten principles. I'm sure you will also learn some new things as well, but keep in mind that this book is just one stone on the path to success. Book after book, experience after experience, sale after sale, put one foot in front of the other. One day, you'll wake up to find yourself living the life you dreamed!

Happy Sales,
Erik Wilt

CHAPTER 1

Preparation – Service Mindset

MOST PEOPLE LOOK FOR EXPERIENCE in the person from whom they take advice. These days, we diligently search the Internet for credible teachers who can help us do everything from lose weight to better understand our spouse to fix a leaky faucet. Often we look for sage advice by checking the newest technology only to feel that when we find the information we've been seeking, it's full of holes. We find ourselves struggling to make the problem fit the solution only to end up causing a bigger mess than that with which we started. Humans have a unique ability to make things way more complicated than they need to be.

Like many other people, I have struggled my way through a sales career. I spent a great deal of time and money trying to learn how to do it better than anyone else. I could cite chapter and verse of the "Sales Bible," but in spite of all my studying, I still had some difficult days. I've been up one day and down the next. I've had managers sing my praises for my sales totals on Monday and then faced trash talk about a failed deal on Wednesday. I've watched cheaters accept awards and I've felt the warm envy that goes hand in hand with a competitive sales culture. There were times when my family could barely make ends meet and other seasons when we spent money like Rockefellers.

Through all of this, I have learned that I love sales; I always will. But love is difficult sometimes. I was looking for a way to even out the peaks and valleys of the sales roller coaster. I searched for anything that might make things just a bit easier—any book, method, or approach that might help calm the waters. Frustration began to set in when I was confronted by an ever-increasing amount of material steering me in so many different directions. They all promised sales mastery and easy results but came at a huge cost. If I had a nickel for every nickel I spent on crappy sales training, I could comfortably retire and put this whole thing behind me!

Don't get me wrong—there are some great techniques out there that use real, effective principles to teach solid sales techniques. But what most of it comes down to is new packaging of the same old stuff. There is no silver bullet or magic pill. There is still work for you to do. This book will not solve all your problems overnight either. It won't make sales easier but it will clear the clutter and make your work simpler. You will still meet prospects you can't close and you will still spend painful hours working on impossible deals. There will still be difficult days. But this book can help; it serves a different purpose entirely.

If you haven't put the book down yet, you probably appreciate honesty. If that's the case, I want to encourage you to keep reading. The real goal of this book isn't to fool you into thinking that a career in sales is easy; it is challenging just like anything that's worth doing. But the purpose of this book is to serve as a road map to help simplify your journey. It is always easier to accomplish something when you've got a good map. After all, Sir Edmund Hillary knew the trek up to the summit of Mount Everest wasn't going to be easy, but charting his journey made things a whole lot simpler. It is my sincere hope that after reading this book, you will discover that you are already in possession of the abilities you need to be successful in sales but that with the right road map, you can chart your best course.

There Is Nothing New under the Sun

A few years back, I was working in sales for a company and decided to play a little joke on a friend of mine. I had a knack for cold calling and I was pretty good at booking a lot of sales appointments. My friend, I'll call him Peter, was struggling on the phones. We were both working from the same Excel file on Peter's computer and were sitting next to each other. I booked my last appointment right before lunch. I stood up to stretch and I noticed the worn-out, emotionally exhausted look on Peter's face. I wanted to help him but I also couldn't resist messing with him a little.

"Peter," I asked, "why so down?"

"I *hate* these phones!" he said. "I can't get an appointment to save my life!"

"Hold on," I told him. "I think I may have something that might help." I opened the Excel file that we had been working from and I changed the font to Gothic. I knew if I printed out the list in a different font, he might think it was a different list of potential customers. I had the bait to set the trap.

"Have you ever paid management for the Platinum Leads before?" I asked. "They're game-changers when you need to book your appointments really fast."

Peter hung on every word. His eyes got wide. "No one told me about those! How much are they?"

"Well," I said, ruffling the papers in my hand, "the cost varies. I get just enough so I can book my appointments fast. I don't like to spend a lot of money on leads." I stopped and pecked at the keys on my laptop as if I was opening up a different file. "Okay," I said, "I have some leftovers here I could part with for ten bucks. That way you can see if you really like them. How does that sound? Are you in?"

"Oh yeah!" Peters said. He practically squealed with delight.

I hit print and ran off to the printer. When I got back Peter told me he was a couple of bucks short. I told him to take the list and pay me when he had the cash.

A friend who had been listening to our exchange from his cubicle next door leaned around the corner and mouthed, "No way!" He couldn't believe this rookie kid had fallen for my lame prank. Peter grabbed the list out of my hands and began punching in phone numbers with excitement.

Two minutes later he had an appointment. Two minutes after that he had another one. Just before lunch he finished booking his day and seemed like he was floating two feet off the ground. It was the perfect time to break the news.

I clapped my hand on his shoulder and told him what I'd done in front of the whole office. Peter's face turned red but he laughed it off. After all, he'd managed to book all his appointments! We all had a great laugh and Peter told me the lesson he'd learned was priceless; there are no special leads or secret systems. There is hard work, basic sales fundamentals, and a new belief that made all the difference.

It's Simple but It Ain't Easy

When I finally ran out of steam trying to find the silver bullet or the secret sauce to make sales easier, I stopped searching and hit the bricks, followed the system, hit my goals, and got paid. And I realized there is no other way. A sales career is just like any other. Some people get into it to see if they have a special talent for it, but most give up when the going gets tough. Many people get into sales thinking they can make an easy buck, and while it *can* be simple to make money in sales, it's definitely *not* easy.

There is a misconception about sales that those who choose it as a profession are only in it for the money. But that's not true at all. In fact, the goal of sales is very simple: help as many people as possible. Chances are, if you like to help people get what they need or solve problems, you would enjoy a career in sales. You may think that you're not a good salesperson but the reality is that we all sell to each other all the time. Don't fool yourself. Likely all you need is a few minor adjustments and a decent road map, and before you know it, you'll be selling with the best of them. This road map can help seasoned sales veterans, those brand new to the craft, or others wanting to gain some basic knowledge about sales alike. Either way, you're in the right place.

Genesis: The First Sale

The biblical account of creation is an interesting one. Whether you believe it to be literal or allegorical, there are some incredible principles to be learned from the story. One thing that stood out to me is the fact that God was actually the first salesperson. This was a pretty shocking realization, considering the perception most people have of salespeople is something other than holy, but it's true! God began by creating an incredible product. According to the story, he created light, earth, water, stars, the moon, sea life, and all the animals on earth—basically the whole enchilada. Then he creates man and makes the first sale, during which no money changes hands. God and man enter into a gentlemen's agreement, if you will. God offers man dominion over everything if he agrees to tend it. Creating and then selling, God is truly the divine entrepreneur.

Value, Not Cost

The first principle we can learn from this story is that sales is less about cost and more about value. In the story, something incredible was created that could be enjoyed. Instead of the creator putting a price tag on his creation in order to make a profit, the creation was offered to someone who could both enjoy and care for it. A good foundation makes for a strong building, and when we approach sales the same way, we can create a strong foundation of trust with our customers.

Here's another way to look at it: I love coffee and I know that I can get an industrial-sized can of Colombian coffee for the same price as the small package of my favorite brand, Peet's. I tried buying the can once to save a little money but I could barely choke it down. I had to add cream, sugar, *and* cinnamon just to make it palatable. When I finished that swamp water, I vowed never to cheat on Peet again. This isn't just a coffee snob's lament either. What I realized is that Peet spent time perfecting his roasting and blending techniques so that his coffee would appeal to a specific group of people, but so did the folks who put out that can of Colombian sludge. I don't want to add cream, sugar, and cinnamon to my coffee because I want to actually be able to taste the coffee, but there are plenty of folks out there who doctor up their coffee every morning. These people likely don't care as much about the flavor profile of the actual beans, and despite my feelings on the canned coffee, that's absolutely fine. We all value different things and when we offer something that someone finds value in, it makes everyone happy. What we did is solve a problem by providing something that someone wanted. By doing that, we left that person happier than we found them. That is selling!

The Genesis story nails this principle. Salespeople need to be passionate about what they offer. In the story, God offers mankind something of incredible value. The story tells us that God saw his creation and said it was good. And God is, you know, God, so it must have been pretty sweet! Because God was passionate about the product, the customer became passionate about it as well. The customer—in this case mankind—saw the value in the offer and became excited and passionate as well. Many salespeople sell products or services they don't believe in for high commissions, but most eventually resign with regrets. I have been there. I have tried to sell things that I wasn't passionate about while justifying myself by making good money, but in the end, passion is always going to trump cash. Cash won't last. Be sure to find something of value that you can be passionate about so that when you offer it, you can do so from your heart.

There is also something else we need to take into consideration when discussing sales and value: benefits. When God made his divine offer, mankind was no different than the rest of what God created. By taking what was offered, mankind was given something to enjoy and to be responsible for. In this case, the buyer was buying the benefits and assuming the responsibility.

Another story comes to mind that helps to illustrate this benefit principle. I remember running down the stairs of a twelve-story office building in Denver with another salesman one cold winter day. "Oh no! Here she comes," I said, "Let's take the stairs!"

We were running from the most aggressive salesperson at the company and she had dollar signs in her eyes. She'd been harassing the whole office about donating to a fund-raiser for a ski program her kid wanted to participate in. It had absolutely nothing to do with work but we knew how good a salesperson she was. My friend and I knew that if we could get out into the cold, we would lose her because she never dressed for the weather. We had already donated twenty bucks each, so we didn't feel bad about dodging her this time. That, and we have learned from a mutual friend that she could have easily footed the bill for her son's ski program herself but she was so cheap that she tried to shake down the whole office instead.

Later that day at the office, she ended up catching me alone. She pressed me hard for the money but I stood my ground. I resisted her charms and told her no. With a dejected look on her face, she asked why I wouldn't donate. Instead of reminding her I had already done so, I told her that I couldn't see the benefit. She started to remind me in a smug tone that it would benefit her child but stopped in the middle of her explanation. I could see the light of realization spread across her face. For the first time, she could see how important it is to communicate the benefit to the buyer instead of pressing her sales agenda.

If a crucial part of the foundation of sales is offering something we feel passionate about, then the other part is to offer it to someone who will see the benefit. This might seem like a no-brainer, but average salespeople ignore major implications when they don't consider this principle. You can even take the story above as proof that you can be a top salesperson when you offer opportunity to people without considering the benefit. The reality is that the star saleswoman was a legend for a day when she pushed a big sale through and was scraping together the pieces of her failed cases as time marched on. She was always scrambling to backfill failed cases with new cases that she could force through. Like Esau, who infamously sold his birthright for some stew in the Old Testament, her short-sighted business model focused on *her* benefit, not the benefit of the client. Over time, she had to pay back tens of thousands of dollars in commissions for failed deals. While she was applauded for some large deals, she ended up with an average income due to the cases that fell through the cracks. Her unethical model was focused on short-term success, so her success was fleeting. In two years' time, she found herself untrusted, alone, and on the fast track to losing her job. She had her chance to learn and decided to sell her birthright instead. When a salesperson is passionate about what they offer and force it on people who don't benefit, that behavior defines the pushy, agenda-driven characters we all loathe.

So many people with good intentions jump into a sales career with the intention of doing good things for their family, their community, and themselves, but they lose sight of those intentions as selfish agendas form around their desire for success. A salesperson suffers a disconnect from their good intentions when their agendas make potential prospects feel insignificant. Potential buyers are repulsed when they are made to feel insignificant, so to make up for that, we begin to push for more and more and bigger and bigger numbers. This is why sales is somewhat of a paradox. Salespeople set out to offer people something they are excited about that they know will show obvious benefits to many, but they forget that not everyone will buy. But when they finally come face to face with those prospects, the goal of closing a sale with maximum benefit to the prospect gets fuzzy. When we let our mental agenda cloud our judgment, we get impatient with people who are genuinely trying to decide if our offer is something they can't live without. The exchange can get tense, and if a prospect feels pressure, they can pull back. This is why it is especially important to keep the value and benefits to the prospect in mind. Financial success will follow, but it should never be the driving factor.

Art and Science

Because it is important for us as salespeople to balance our intense passion about our offerings with our duty to make the benefits obvious to our prospects, we find ourselves in the pursuit of both art and science. The mind serves as both our canvas and a crucible. We communicate with the passion of an artist by telling stories and painting pictures, while at the same time using facts and research to summarize the benefits of our offerings. A good salesperson walks the sales tightrope with precision and grace. They must keep both the product and the prospect in mind. It's a true juggling act, one only the most devoted and skilled salespeople can master.

What a noble place to begin! If we choose to look at it this way, we truly have an opportunity to do God's work. The example from Genesis highlights the communication between God and mankind and illustrates the origins of the first sale. This illustration is the perfect example for us to look to as we work to craft our own personal approach to sales. We must be always mindful to avoid building an offer on the shaky foundation of a personal agenda. Remember: the point of the sale is not to do what's right for you alone. Truly, every sale is a relationship. If we do it right, it becomes a love-centered relationship.

My love of coffee having already been established, I have another story that illustrates this concept. Growing up in Oregon I learned to enjoy coffee earlier than many people. At sixteen, I found myself at a very busy coffee shop I had never been to before early one Sunday morning. The line was long, as eager churchgoers stopped in to grab coffee and pastries on their way to worship. Standing in line, I looked around for the usual menu board to decide what I wanted before I reached the register.

When my turn finally came, I found myself face to face with a barista, frozen in indecision. The name Matty was embroidered in white script on his green shirt. He grinned at me and asked what I would like.

"Uh," I stammered, cognizant of the long line behind me, "do you have a menu?"

"It doesn't really work that way," he said, still smiling. "What do you like?"

"Well, coffee," I explained, "And, uh, pastries?"

Perhaps taking pity on me, he began to ask additional questions. "Do you like almond?"

"Sure," I said.

"What about cherry?"

"Yeah," I said, "I practically live off Cherry Coke."

Matty's smile grew and he stepped back. With confidence he declared, "I shall blow your mind!"

For the next few minutes, I watched him froth, mix, steam, pour, and concoct what he seemed certain would be a life-changing elixir. Finally, he placed the cup in front of me and begged me to try it.

He seemed genuinely interested in my reaction. Compelled by his confidence and his mastery as a barista, I took a sip and my life changed.

Contrary to what you might be thinking, it wasn't the drink itself that changed my life. The drink was fine, mediocre perhaps, but the service was unmatched. The service is what inspired me to change up my morning routine and make that particular coffee shop a regular stop. Over the following weeks, I became great friends with Matty as I stopped in for coffee. Southern Oregon is not hurting for coffee shops and there were hundreds of other places I could have spent my money—some of them may have even served better drinks—but none of those places had Matty. Matty and I have been friends for over twenty years now and it all started with that single sale.

Matty put love and passion into serving people. Sure, good service meant that he would make better tips, but he never knew who the big tippers were, so he had to give everyone the same level of great service. When he took that approach, people started to tip him with their hard-earned dollars based on the value he added to their morning, not the cost of the drink.

I learned a great deal about sales from Matty. I learned that as salespeople, serving from our hearts and seeking to present our offerings with passion can be transformative. Any objections to cost disappear like magic in the shadow of heartfelt concern. I didn't ask Matty how much his life-changing drink was going to cost; it didn't matter. He wanted to make me happy and give me something I wanted. I was his target prospect. Likewise, we must stop wasting time with people who won't benefit from what we have to offer. Had I gone in there looking for a simple, black coffee, I most likely would not have been receptive to Matty's questions. You have to know your customer.

Do not sell people that which they do not need. You've heard the expression "He's so good he can sell a ketchup Popsicle to a women in white gloves"? To do so is no longer a badge of accomplishment. Sell the customer only what he or she needs and can benefit from.

Nothing Happens Until Somebody Sells Something

Peter Drucker, the modern management guru, believed that sales were vital to society. But he balanced that belief with a key idea: a company's primary responsibility is to serve its customers. That means that one of the greatest business thinkers of our time believed in sales but put serving the customer as priority one!

This flies in the face of what we've been told by old-school sales managers and hotshot salespeople! Gone are the days of a company calling all the shots while forcing shoddy products out the doors to be sold by pushy salespeople to customers who don't want them in the first place. The sales environment has shifted; people now expect simple needs to be met by engaging people who want to earn their business honestly and who are genuinely interested in helping their clients.

The rise of the online sales marketplace—particularly with websites like Amazon and eBay—has caused much discussion about whether or not the role of the traditional sales professional is dying. To that I say, "I hope so!" The new salesperson for this new age will need to have both a heart and a sharper focus. This new salesperson will offer products and services they believe in and they will do it in a way that establishes real value. Gone are the days of moving units solely for profit; it's now time to move hearts and minds.

Summary

Sales truly can be divine work. Remember the example from Genesis of the first sale. If we take this model and apply it to sales philosophy, we will find ourselves creating lasting relationships of mutual benefit that will last longer than any career. Perhaps we can all find a Matty of our very own! Our desire to offer what we have will come from the heart and we won't ruin relationships by forcing a quick sale on everyone we meet, regardless of need. This genuine interest in helping others will spawn new relationships that will, in turn, bear fruit. People naturally want to help those whom they like. And isn't being helped better than being called "pushy" behind your back?

By establishing a strong foundation built on an ethical sales philosophy crafted with passion and benefit, we can build an entire sales system, leading to a successful career, the first step on the road to a successful life.

CHAPTER 2

Endurance – Success Mindset

Everybody thinks of changing humanity,
but nobody thinks of changing himself.
—Leo Tolstoy

I HAVE OFTEN DREAMED about spending time in the minds of great thinkers for a day. The opportunity to see life through the eyes of Abraham Lincoln, Steve Jobs, or Dale Carnegie really appeals to me. The most inviting aspect is the chance to understand the thought processes of these vaunted thinkers. What kinds of things were going through their minds as they fought successfully to change the world? These people were particularly gifted at amassing huge armies of supporters who believed in their ideologies and approaches. At times, their appeal was almost messianic. In most cases, these great thinkers revolutionized their field and did great things for many people. To know and understand their beliefs may not magically transform us into visionaries, but I'm willing to bet it would teach us a lot about ourselves.

If we look at the people who have changed the world in the face of incredible adversity, we often find the common thread of choosing his or her mindset. Every great world changer throughout history established and maintained a mindset to transcend the adversity he or she faced. Choosing how we react to fear and the attitude we maintain has the greatest impact on our mindset.

Because most of us aren't working on crafting a legacy that tilts the world on its axis, the idea of working on our mindset can seem like a waste of time. We may use any number of excuses to avoid confronting our preconceived beliefs and assumptions, but the real reason we avoid it is fear. "What if I start working on my mindset and I become someone I don't like?" we ask. "What if I decide that what I previously thought is wrong?" Nobody likes to realize they're wrong. "If I create a mindset where I'm wildly successful, that might mean more responsibility and I already feel worn out!" All of these are common questions, but the common root in all of them is fear.

What would your life look like without fear? Our days might be cut short as we took life-threatening risks. We would stand numb in the presence of opportunity. Fear can push us to safety or motivate us to conquer. Without fear, we might try petting a mountain lion or fighting a UFC fighter. But without fear we would never fight the good fight. Fear pushes us to make decisions for self-preservation or to subdue threats. Without fear we would be doomed.

Fear is a powerful emotion. It's used to sell us everything from acne cream to political candidates. And it's something with which we have become so intimately familiar that we don't even realize when it's being used against us anymore. When we were younger, we were aware of fear. It was visceral, and vivid and we always knew when we were scared. The world was new and we had to learn the difference between rational and irrational fears. As we are subjected to scary movies, parental warnings, and the fear of rejection, fear is all around us; sometimes it's even more common than love. It's become so prevalent that we've lost that sense of noticing when we're afraid.

The Case for Fear

To understand fear we can look at potential coping options. When a child senses fear, he or she reacts. There is the fight-or-flight response. A confident child will fight what he or she fears because he or she believes there is a good chance he or she might win. If the danger is too great the decision to flee will make the most sense. These two simple options have worked for eons; they are embedded in our psyche. But there is a third option: suppression. Fear suppression is handled by the amygdala in our brain. A study conducted at Rutgers University verified that the brain can dampen fear so that greater risks can be taken for self-preservation. Suppression of fear makes sense only in the case of self-preservation, but in today's atmosphere of fear, suppression has become the drug of choice.

Fighting and running aren't expedient reactions in our modern world. Society pushes us to maintain a stiff upper lip and endure hardness. We are raised to be good citizens solving problems in civilized ways, not by fighting or fleeing. From an early age almost everyone is taught to stifle fear and get back in line. The result is legions of disenfranchised citizens. We have become a mass of people who are afraid to act when confronted with fear and we have no clue why we feel restrained.

As a child, I was afraid of the dark. I remember lying awake on the bottom bunk wrapped in my Teenage Mutant Ninja Turtles comforter and my E.T. sheets. I gripped the blanket tightly as I tried to keep my eyes squeezed shut. My heart started beating hard as my fear grew. At the time, I didn't understand the physiological reactions my body was undergoing but now I realize I was pumping adrenaline into my blood stream. My temples pounded and I began to sweat. My body was telling me to run to my parent's room but my brain was ordering me to toughen up. My six-year-old muscles locked up and finally, I screamed! I screamed like my life depended on it. Sadly, it would not be the last time.

This was the first time I remember being truly afraid while fighting to suppress my fear, and I bring it up because it's important. That experience has shaped my conception of fear and my expectations about how I cope with my fears. By suppressing fear instead of reacting freely to it, my experience coping with fear was torturous. It reinforced my resolve to avoid the things I was afraid of for many years. That's how we adopt the habit of running from our fears. It's the mindset regarding fear that matters. We need to be free to react in a positive way toward fear because fear is a catalyst for action.

We're Off to See the Wizard

Another fearful experience was inspired by something you would never expect to cause such an intense reaction. My father, in an effort to bond with me, took me to see *Gremlins* at the movie theater. He wasn't trying to scare me; he just wanted to spend some time with me, and I had begged him to see the movie. Now, if I had known how scared I would be, I would never have lobbied so hard, but that's not how fear works. No one who boarded the *Titanic* thought about icebergs. Fear almost always starts out looking like a good time.

My father didn't dampen my excitement by telling me that the movie would scare me. He did not ensure that I would be up all night in fear of a tiny monster taking a bite out of me. And even though that's exactly what happened, I'm glad I hadn't been forewarned. We need to live looking forward to what's next and hoping for great outcomes. Living authentically means not worrying about the potential monster around every corner. Taking an unknown path can mean great things. Robert Frost's most famous poem, "The Road Not Taken," is about this very thing! We cannot let fear of what might happen dull our experiences.

We spend much of our lives following interesting paths in a desire to explore. With great anticipation and excitement, we seek out the unknown. But sometimes we turn the corner and run into a bear. Then fear sets in.

Even so, we must never lose that hunger for adventure and excitement. There is nothing wrong with being excited. Too many people try to get through their days without getting excited because they don't want to get their hopes up. Every potentially exciting thing is couched in cautious optimism, thereby dulling the effect. Everything we really want is just on the other side of what we fear.

Oops, I Did It Again

Every time we experience genuine fear, we are also hit by feelings of naïveté and embarrassment. There is always the belief that we should have known better. "How could I have been so oblivious?" we ask ourselves. This is our way of punishing ourselves for thinking we could find adventure and excitement by trying something new. This happened to my six-year-old self as well.

The lights were out but the bedroom door was open a crack to allow some outside lights to stream in. I remember beating myself up for trying to prove I was a big boy by sitting through the entire movie even though dad had offered to leave early once he realized I was frightened. I began to punish myself mentally.

When our blood starts pumping faster and the adrenaline courses through our veins, the mental punishments we inflict on ourselves come faster and faster. We get a surge of energy and our fight-or-flight response kicks in. Sucked up into this emotional and physical vortex, we often freeze when our body is telling us to flee. Meanwhile, our rational brains are turned off and we don't for a moment consider that that which we fear isn't real.

It's obvious that there is no such thing as a gremlin but to a six-year-old, fact and fiction can blur. My fear of gremlins was based in realistic things that I had experienced. I thought the fur on Gizmo, the good gremlin, was like a hamster; his scaly skin after he transformed reminded me of a lizard or snake. The gremlin moved like an animal and all the humans in the movie reacted to it as though it were real. As far as I was concerned, it was! This complicated mix of real familiarities combined with Hollywood magic confuses our brain's ability to respond. This kind of confusion at such a young age can reverberate and greatly affect how we approach our fears in adulthood.

Time to Change the Channel

Instead of being frozen in fear like a six-year-old boy in his movie theater seat, a successful mindset requires a different approach. What we don't realize is that when this cycle of fear begins, it is easy to cut it short and create maximum impact toward positive change instead. The moment you feel that surge of energy and anxiety about taking the next step, making that phone call, or approaching someone, do it anyway! Don't waste all of your precious energy on negative thoughts that end up causing paralysis. Fear exists but we are in control. Your body is doing one of the best things it knows how to do; it is giving you superhuman powers so you can conquer your fear. Don't waste that gift.

As a little kid, I gave in to the fear and had to spend decades working to unlearn my automatic response to fear. I'm sure it will be a struggle for me for the rest of my life. That energy channeled itself into years of anxiety. My coping mechanism was made worse by the shame I felt in uncomfortable situations around friends. Fear was holding me captive because I was allowing it to take over by trying to suppress it. When we resign and let fear win, it can ruin us in major ways. The good news is we don't have to do it.

It may not seem like it, but we are actually in control. We can release the energy from fear and channel it into action. We can turn that fear into motivation, a game changer for any sales career. Attacking fear and facing it head on is a foolproof way to jump-start any pursuit. This is the sticking point for the vast majority of salespeople who claim they are in a sales slump. They are afraid and they have internalized that fear. Progress has come to a screeching halt.

Keep Your Friends Close and Your Enemies Closer

While the suppression of fear is the enemy of progress, we can make the appearance of fear work for us. We can almost use fear as a barometer, telling us when we're about to hit it big. When we enter a scary scenario and our adrenaline starts pumping, we can perform at a very high level. Think about athletes who talk about playing through pain because of adrenaline. It happens to all of us. I have experienced it in my own life. I have knocked on doors, called people I didn't know, and chatted with millionaires only to find out that none of them were the least bit scary. I've asked for and received checks for hundreds of thousands of dollars from clients. No one slammed the door in my face or kicked me out of their house. I did things I was afraid of because I learned how to make fear my ally.

To make fear work for you, think back to a time when you were afraid and relive the moment. Maybe you've jumped in a freezing body of water? Gone skydiving? Bungee jumping? These are all very scary things that many of us nevertheless choose to do.

I remember jumping from a bridge into Applegate Lake when I was growing up. My first attempt was with a friend named Scott. He was older and much cooler than me. He liked Bob Marley, mountain biking, and jumping off bridges into cold lakes! We drove up to the lake and parked in a dirt pullout next to the bridge. Before I knew it, Scott was running full-speed at the guardrail, screaming like a madman. He leaped and launched his body into the air without ever checking to see if there was water in the lake. I heard him scream for what seemed like way too long and heard a splash; I ran to the edge to check on him. I couldn't believe what I saw. After a blind thirty-five-foot plunge into Applegate Lake, Scott treaded water and yelled, "Come on, man! The water is amazing!" I carefully climbed over the edge and stared down at the water. No way was I going to chicken out in front of this cool kid. My adrenaline was pumping and Scott yelled something I will never forget. "If you think about it, you won't do it!" he said. Simple and profound; I jumped.

When my head broke the surface, Scott was screaming praises at the top of his lungs. I felt like I could conquer anything. Together we made our way back up the embankment and jumped over and over again for hours. Sometimes we would add tricks and when girls showed up, we would try to impress them by running past their boyfriends and doing blind jumps as the other guys cowered on the edge of the bridge. By channeling my adrenaline into action I had the time of my life, built instant rapport with someone I respected, gained confidence to try other things that scared me, and stood out from my peers.

Sometimes, when I face something that makes my palms sweat, I go back to that bridge. Sometimes I even tell myself, "Bombs away!" which reminds me of the time I used fear to my advantage. You can do this too. Work to cultivate confidence and stand out by doing that which you fear. With the right mindset, you will find yourself a top salesperson before you know it.

Attitude: That Little Thing That Makes a Big Difference

If conquering fear is half the battle, attitude is the other half. There are plenty of people who fear nothing but who have a terrible attitude. We see them on our morning commute and in grocery store parking lots. I call them bad drivers. We can learn a lot from bad drivers. For instance, I learned that attitude is highly transferable when I was driving down the street one day and noticed that the lane on my right ended in merge arrows. My own lane was slowing to a stop because someone ahead was waiting to make a left. In my side mirror, I saw the headlights of a car about six cars back moving into the merge lane. Driving like Mario Andretti, the driver flew up next to me, braked, and started blowing his horn. He rolled down his window and started blowing his top. "Get out of the way, (expletive)!" he yelled. I couldn't quite believe he was talking to me but he *was* looking right at me. "I can't move," I said, gesturing to the line of cars ahead of me. In response, he flipped me off and looked for the next break in the line of cars. As the car ahead of me began to move, he wedged his way and flipped me the bird one more time. I didn't really think a lot of it; bad drivers are just part of everyday life. But when I got home I found myself being short with the kids and Linsey. Even though I'd had a pretty good day, I was negative about it. I felt off the whole evening. I let that bad driver's bad attitude ruin most of my evening.

In sales, we work around and in collaboration with colleagues. Sometimes we have a Debby Downer in the mix. You know the type. You come in the office fully caffeinated and ready to change the world when you hear the office door slam; then you hear a brief-case hit the floor. Maybe you hear a deep sigh three cubicles away. No one has said anything but you can feel the tension in the air; the whole office is walking on eggshells. Imagine what that does to the person who has to sit next to the Negative Nancy.

The Tale of the Wyoming Garden Fork

I was working as an insurance agent in Wyoming with a person who exemplified positive attitude. We were working in Cheyenne, which is a great town, but like any place else, if you looked for something to complain about, you could find it.

I had come to enjoy working in Cheyenne and always looked forward to training a new agent there. The drive usually took about two hours each way and we would work twelve-hour days. We worked hard to communicate value to the working-class people of Cheyenne. It was a great proving ground to challenge the attitude and perception of any new salesperson.

The saleswoman I was with, I'll call her Carrie, was experienced but new to a career in insurance. She had a seemingly endless supply of positive attitude and the energy of the Energizer bunny. Just to get a laugh, Carrie would tell people a fictitious story about her father getting a huge delivery of horse manure delivered to her family farm when she was growing up; she claimed her father caught her digging in the manure. Her father asked what she was doing. "Looking for the pony of course!" she said. "With a pile of manure that big there has to be a pony in here somewhere!" The story always got a laugh and her attitude inspired me.

One windy day in Cheyenne, we made our way to the front gate of another appointment. The homeowner was digging in his front yard with some gardening tools. As we walked up to the gate he rushed over to us, garden fork in the air. "I know you all are here to sell insurance, but I'm not interested so just get on out of here!" I'm persistent but not stupid and I figured if this cowboy was going to stick that fork in me for coming to his gate, I wasn't about to push it any further.

Taking a step back, I started a conversation that I still remember today. "What's got you so riled up today?" I asked, even though I was fearful of what he might do.

He stopped in his tracks and looked at us nervously. "You all didn't say you were going to sell me insurance on the phone when you made the appointment and I don't want any!"

"Well that may or may not be true," I said, "but can I ask you another question?" He nodded. "What in the world do you plan on doing with that garden fork in your hand?" I smiled. "You gonna eat me with it?"

He looked down and began chuckling at himself. "I don't know," he said. "Sorry about that; I was just mad is all."

The man smiled and looked over at Carrie, who started to chuckle too. Seeing that we weren't likely to make a sale but at least we wouldn't be impaled by a gardening fork, I said, "Well, I definitely won't offer you any insurance, but there's nothing you can do that will get me to stop liking you. You made our day!" At that, he burst into a deep Cheyenne cowboy laugh.

"Good luck to you all!" he said as we hopped in our car and headed off to our next appointment. I can't remember if we sold anything the rest of that day but it doesn't matter. The difference a positive attitude makes might not seem important in the moment, but it's the difference between getting on your horse one more time and hanging up your hat.

Carrie had been modeling a positive attitude the whole time we struggled through Cheyenne. Getting up at 4:30 a.m. to drive two hours, inhale methane for most of the day (the oil and gas industry is a major employer in Cheyenne), and get chased by a cowboy with a garden fork would be more than enough to turn anyone off. Not Carrie. She could always find the pony in the pile of manure; she taught me how as well.

Conquer the Self

"If you do not conquer self, you will be conquered by self," said Napoleon Hill, author of *Think and Grow Rich*. When examining the mindset of a successful salesperson, there are two factors that stand out: fear and attitude. Both of these factors influence our behavior but they are both also subject to our will. We will experience fear but we can choose how to respond. Our attitude may be challenged but we can decide to approach the situation negatively or to "look for the pony."

A positive attitude is not something immediately available to you from the beginning. Like any skill, it's honed over time. To build a positive mindset, you have to approach it like a weight-training program. You have to train hard. We can train our minds in the same way by focusing on three specific things.

1. **Who we spend time with.** Attitudes are shared easily between friends; so are fears, dreams, goals, and other beliefs. A rising tide lifts all ships. Famed entrepreneur Jim Rohn said that we are the average of the five people we spend the most time with. Are you spending time with people who are positive, hardworking, and relentless for success? Or are they negative, skeptical, doubtful, and driven by fear? Start surrounding yourself with people in control of their attitudes and who possess a positive outlook.

2. **What we see and hear.** I could have avoided years of fear had I decided to walk out of the movie theater with my father when I was six instead of insisting that I was a big boy. When we give in to ego and self-promotion, we encourage new fears. When we allow for self-indulgence and carelessness, our positive attitude erodes. What life philosophies are you listening to? What kinds of music or movies do you watch? It may seem trivial but what you consume—even passively—has a huge effect on your attitude toward life.

3. **What we say.** What we say about ourselves, others, and our life tends to come true. Our speech is often a self-fulfilling prophecy. Self-talk plays a huge role in the creation of our attitude and our ability to face our fears. Consequently, our

attitude dictates our behavior. Our behavior is what creates our results and those results feed back into what we say about ourselves. For example, if I say I am becoming a better salesperson because I am learning more about sales every day, my attitude about my ability will improve. When my attitude about my sales ability improves, I become more effective at utilizing what I have been learning. By using what I have been learning, I close more sales, which confirms what I said about myself to begin with. We can make the cycle of positivity work for us!

CHAPTER 3

Stepping Out – Prospecting Mindset

First Day of School

MEETING PEOPLE DOESN'T COME EASY for everyone. Some people are naturals, while others struggle. Recently, it was the first day of school in southern Oregon where I live. Our house is close enough to the elementary school that the kids can walk. Most of the family was excited about the new school year. My kids were excited to walk to school, catch up with their friends, meet their teachers, and use the new playground. Jonathan, the third of our four children, was the only holdout. He lumbered down the sidewalk several steps behind everyone else. He was clearly upset but trying to maintain a stiff upper lip. He didn't want my wife, Linsey, and I to worry. I knew he was telling himself that he wasn't allowed to be afraid. After all, he was in fourth grade now!

Noticing Jonathan lagging behind, I slowed my walk to match his pace and asked him a few questions. "Hey, buddy," I said, "Why so down?"

"I'm fine," he replied and stared straight ahead, watching his little brother bounce from driveway to driveway, making machine gun noises.

"You don't seem fine," I prodded. "Did you get enough breakfast?"

"Yeah, I'm fine," he said again. "Don't worry about me, Dad."

"Okay," I shrugged, "you just aren't acting like yourself. I thought you were excited about today!"

He didn't reply; he just kept walking. I left him to his solitary walk and caught up with Linsey. We chatted about how things had gone that morning and tried to remember if anything had happened that might have put Jonathan in a bad mood; we couldn't think of anything. We kept walking, and as we got closer to the school, the other kids got more excited as Jonathan became more irritated with them.

We stopped and I knelt down to look him in the eyes. "Are you nervous, buddy?" I asked. I watched the weight of the world drop from his shoulders. He nodded his head and I watched him choke back tears. "Oh, buddy," I said, my heart breaking for my son, "it's okay to be nervous. I'm nervous for you! Do you think you need to be special or try to make as many friends as possible?" I asked as I hugged him tightly.

"Yeah," he admitted. "I know that's what you want me to do. I just don't feel like talking to a bunch of people. I'd rather play alone today," he mumbled into my shoulder. "I just feel more comfortable that way."

In my excitement I had unknowingly put too much pressure on him to make friends and enjoy school. I had failed to realize that we all approach social situations differently. I like to jump in with both feet and start swimming, assuming I'll figure things out as I go. Jonathan is different; he likes to get the lay of the land and listen for a while before he engages.

I held him by the shoulders and looked at him proudly. "You just take your time and enjoy your day at school the best you can," I said. "You don't have to talk to anyone and you can play by yourself if you want. We love you just the way you are. Okay?"

"Okay, Dad," he said, his anxiety relieved. "Thanks."

We finished the walk to school, snapped a few first-day pictures and watched the children bounce away to their classes. I was glad that I had been able to reach Jonathan by letting him know that his approach to things was absolutely fine and that he didn't have to meet anyone else's standards. I don't always do the right thing as a parent, but when I do, I can't get enough of the feeling.

Jonathan came home that day telling us that his teacher was the best he'd ever had. He said that he finished all his homework at school and he even met a blonde girl he has a crush on and asked her for a private game of wall ball. Things sure seemed to be getting serious!

Believe it or not, this story has everything to do with prospecting. In sales we meet people all the time. That is what we do. Salespeople get paid for two things: prospecting and presenting.

For most people, prospecting is the activity they fear the most. However, it also carries the biggest reward. The phrase "nothing ventured, nothing gained" is surely applicable here. I've worked with war heroes who'd been shot at by Afghani snipers, and I've watched as they stared at the phone for hours, frozen in fear. I've trained bodybuilders accustomed to being critiqued and judged and watched them collapse into tears with a phone in their hands. Everyone approaches these situations differently.

My son's first day of school is an applicable story because it illustrates that we all get nervous before doing something great. Prospecting is something great. Prospecting is the doorway to meeting lifelong clients, being a productive part of the world, and creating a life for our family beyond what we can dream. We don't need to be the best prospector in the world on our first day; we just need to get out on the playground.

The Case for Prospecting

As a new dad, I can remember certain memories more clearly than others. Abigail is our firstborn, and I remember her wild hair, her infatuation with the Doodlebops, and an insatiable appetite for warm milk. There are also memories I wish I could forget. The one that comes to mind is the first time I encountered a diaper blowout. For those of you without children, imagine what happens when a diaper fails at that for which it is designed, and if fails spectacularly. I didn't even know something like that was possible.

When a situation like a diaper blowout occurs, you have two choices: fix it or forget it. As a new dad, I was all for the "forget it" option but the great thing about having a baby is that they have a built-in alarm system. It wasn't long before Abby was alerting us and everyone within earshot to the fact that she wasn't happy. The reasons to fix the problem became more compelling with each passing minute. With the screaming comes the squirming, which is the only warning a parent gets before the mess begins. What took me by surprise was how quickly a bad diaper rash can develop if it's not treated quickly. The rash makes the initial procrastination so much worse because the child can cry in pain for days after the initial problem is fixed. Procrastinating or "forgetting" just exacerbates the problem.

Salespeople look at prospecting the same way new dads look at changing diaper blowouts: forget it! Most salespeople become incredibly good at finding ways to avoid prospecting. I know this firsthand because I've become incredibly creative myself when it comes to avoiding prospecting. I have avoided prospecting by watching YouTube videos, checking Facebook, and responding to emails. I have grabbed a cup of coffee, checked my mailbox, and "asked my manager a question." One person who worked out of my office hated prospecting so much that he took up smoking to justify taking a smoke break so he could avoid calling people. I've watched people practice the call script, organize their call list, and "listen so they can see how it's done." If you want full attendance at a meeting for salespeople, schedule it in the middle of prospecting time; there won't be an empty seat in the room!

You would think management would want to chain salespeople to phones so that prospecting would actually happen. Management has production goals to meet and they can be pressured in big ways to make those numbers, but in spite of that, they insist on getting in the way and putting more obstacles between you and your sales. Meetings, compliance paperwork, evaluations, continuing education, email responses, and conference calls all clutter up your day. Pile on the busy work and watch your paycheck shrink!

I started to log my time to see how much time I was actually spending on income-producing activities. I remember logging a twelve-hour day while my children were on winter break. They called me and begged me to come home so that we could build a gingerbread house together. I declined, finished out my day, and got home in time to tuck them into bed. And yet when I looked at the income-producing time I had logged for the day, it totaled one measly hour! That is when decided to take control.

In sales, you determine your paycheck. It's based on how many people you prospect and present to. It is that simple. If you spend time writing thank you cards while your prospects are able to take your calls, you deserve a small paycheck. If you are keeping up with your Facebook feed or know what the Rock tweeted twenty minutes ago while top producers were talking to real people, you might want to rethink your priorities. Taking ownership of your time is the first and most important thing a salesperson can do. In sales, the person you sit next to is not going to buy your groceries, and your manager won't make your dreams come true. You get paid for meeting people and solving their problems. Everything else is a distraction!

If you are willing to fix the problem, then keep on reading. You don't have to be a superstar; all you need to do is get on the playground. If you can't commit to that, sales probably isn't for you. And don't think that you can be in sales just long enough to get that management position (a manager who can't prospect will be a failure) or just long enough to land that "big fish." You've got to really commit. Give yourself permission to pursue other things that are worth your time. You own each moment, so go out and do what you want.

If you are still reading, your sales career is about to change in a big way. This is because you're willing to do the one thing that the faint of heart run from: you will prospect. When you feel like giving up, you can pick up the phone one more time. When your manager threatens you with your job unless you respond to an important email, you can finish out your prospecting block with no fear. When you see that you have five calls left to make and the urge to run to the restroom strikes, you can dance while you dial and make one more appointment. You can ignore your best friend when he or she tells you about Kim Kardashian's latest tweet. If the president of the United States calls, he or she needs to either make a sales appointment or you will call him or her back later.

As the sales roll in, it will be tempting to let up, but you can't do that. In bad times, you prospect. In good times, you prospect. When products change, you prospect. Prospecting is the lifeblood of your career. You don't even have to be in sales. Businesspeople should live by the same advice. If you aren't prospecting you're dying.

Pipeline of Success

Our bodies are made up of about 65% water. Our brains need water to manufacture hormones and neurotransmitters. It allows us to create saliva for digestion, converts our food to energy, and allows us to flush from our body things that would otherwise kill us. Water helps deliver oxygen to our cells, lubricates our joints, and regulates our body temperature. It's an accepted fact that humans cannot survive without water for more than three days. Water also covers 71% of the earth's surface. You've heard the line from Samuel Taylor Coleridge's epic poem "The Rime of the Ancient Mariner": "Water, water every where / Nor any drop to drink," which is all too true. On this planet of abundance, approximately 790 million people (or 11% of the world's population) don't have access to a significant source of water. As a result, millions of people die annually due to the lack of accessible clean water.

In high school, I wasn't big on water consumption. In southern Oregon where I grew up, I had access to pure, clean tap water whenever I wanted it. Yet in those years, I usually opted for something else: Mountain Dew. I spent my teenage years consuming can after can of the citrusy soda and following it with a 7-Eleven Double Big Gulp. The soda sold in stores was cheaper than bottled water, and to me it made no sense to spend money on water; soda was both cheaper and more delicious.

However, when I had blood work done as a teenager, I was confronted with a shocking reality. My doctor informed me that while most everything else was fine, I was chronically dehydrated. I had always thought you had to be thirsty to be dehydrated, but I learned that wasn't the case. My doctor followed up by advising me to drink six to eight cups of water per day and I looked at him like he was crazy. I told him that there must be something wrong with the test because I drank double that in Mountain Dew and there is no way I could add six to eight more cups of water. He started laughing at me; I didn't know what was so funny.

"The Mountain Dew you're drinking isn't helping you hydrate; it's making it harder for your body to stay hydrated," he explained between laughs. "You need to make water the priority, and then if you want to enjoy a Mountain Dew just DEW it in moderation." Ha, ha! Very funny, Doc!

It was a struggle for years for me to transition into drinking enough water. But these days I drink a lot of water and I feel a lot better. Knowing what we know today, I realize that I wasn't simply dehydrating myself. Mountain Dew made up so much of my diet that I was also malnourishing my body, creating hormonal imbalances, and eroding the effectiveness of my other organs. I just thought I was enjoying a tasty beverage!

There is a connection here: just as I needed to drink more water to bring balance to my body, salespeople and business owners need to prospect more to give themselves a solid foundation in sales. Prospecting is the water of sales; it makes up the majority of our business success. There are millions of businesses out there that are malnourished and dehydrated from the lack of prospecting and every year; many of them die. Some businesses and salespeople get by for years on Mountain Dew prospecting. It seems like good stuff because it's easy and sweet. It's the type of prospecting that bears fruit from offering incentives, coupons, or discounts but people still complain about the cost. Mountain Dew prospecting is for order takers, not serious business owners and salespeople.

So what will happen when we shift our approach, hydrate our business, and cease our reliance on Mountain Dew prospecting? To put it simply, a wellspring of business success! But we must do three things to make it happen.

1. **Cleansing:** How often have you felt like your prospects were stale? I have coached business owners who complain about their lack of prospects or they complain that they keep calling on the same people. The businessperson's attitude starts to stink, the quality of business they do starts to look dirty, and their negativity becomes contagious, affecting those around them.

   Just like water, prospects are not in short supply. The problem is usability and access. By looking for and utilizing multiple sources of water, we can rest assured that a single source won't go dry or become compromised. So often we go back the same well again and again; we build our villages near it and rely on it at the exclusion of everything else. When the well runs dry, we think, "How could this have happened?" In order to grow, you *always* need to be looking for new sources of water.

   The successful businessperson works several wells at once and by doing so can ensure that he or she does not run any particular well dry. Instead of focusing all of one's marketing efforts on a networking group (like Business Network International or your local Chamber of Commerce) start adding new methods of prospecting. Host or attend an industry event, dabble in your sphere of influence, or take up volunteering. Find a referral partner to hand exclusive business to. For example, a carpenter can team up with a plumber and an electrician, which adds a new business pipeline. Increasing a social media presence should be something every businessperson considers as a way to become familiar to your prospects. You can also learn a great deal about your prospects before you even pick up the phone by mining social media. Increasing the amount and variety of prospecting a businessperson does will clean up the flow of any business and wash away bad attitudes and dirty business practices.

2. **Nourishing:** Is your business becoming routine or stuck in a rut? Are your results mediocre at best? Some people are ignorantly happy with mediocre results; I see malnourished businesses everywhere. Those are the businesses that don't want to learn new ways to prospect and have no desire to grow. But everyone has heard the phrase "If you aren't growing, you're dying." Stop believing the lie that we can maintain by holding steady. I didn't think I was harming my body by drinking insane amounts of Mountain Dew, but it was all happening under the surface. If we are in business we *must* constantly be learning and growing in our ability to prospect. You don't need to become an expert overnight, but any effort you make to reach more prospects will translate to growth in ways that will surprise you. By

going door to door and business to business your ability to connect with people will improve exponentially, regardless of whether you make any sales! Prospecting nourishes your whole business.

3. **Regulating**: Salespeople love to say, "It's my slow season." At the end of the year they hang their head in shame as they resign themselves to making the same commission as the previous year. "I thought I would be further along in my business by now!" they say. But a quick examination of their prospecting methods will quickly reveal why they haven't become the top producers they'd hoped to be. I'm always amazed when salespeople are scared to ask for referrals and complain about seasonality. With one new prospecting method they could almost always double their business and never have to worry about seasonality again. Here's the secret: they ask their current client, "Who do you know who is struggling with the same issue?" It sounds simple but I have personally paid for services and purchased products knowing people who could benefit just like I did but I was never asked for the referral. People love to help each other and sales are missed every day if referrals aren't requested. By adding new prospecting pipelines, salespeople will have a regulated and constantly growing business.

I can't stress how important it is to develop a prospecting mindset. For the salesperson who heeds the call and decides to prospect through the pain, success will come naturally. Prospecting is vital; it is the water to the body of our business!

CHAPTER 4

Proper Form – Prospecting (CASUAL)

NOW THAT WE HAVE FIRMLY PLACED prospecting in the forefront of our minds, we can wade deeper into the prospecting waters. There are enough books about prospecting methods to fill a library, so this chapter is not meant to serve as a comprehensive instruction manual on how to prospect. Instead, this chapter will expose you to a formula that will work across many methods so that your pipelines can begin to take shape and you can develop a plan to forge ahead with your business.

If we were examining prospecting models with a great return on investment, we would be remiss to not look at the phone approach. A general rule concerning prospecting is that the more personable the interaction, the more fruitful the outcome. Some salespeople argue for the door-to-door approach while others prefer networking,

ERIK WILT

and the methods for each can vary. But wouldn't it be better if there was a simple formula we could use with any approach to prospecting? Keep reading.

I love telling stories, especially those that illustrate principles. I find stories to be an impactful method of teaching. To that end, I have another story for you.

Hippy Waldo

As I had been instructed, I showed up for my first sales position in Denver in business attire. I was all decked out in a dress shirt, tie, and blue suit, ready to do damage. My sales manager had told me that I would be paired up with the top producer in the region. I was excited to meet him and my manager took a few minutes to prepare me.

"You wouldn't think Jon was our top producer by his looks," he said. "The best way I can describe him is Waldo . . . Hippy Waldo." I looked at my manager, confused. He went on. "Do you remember those kids' books that came out years ago with all the tiny cartoon characters? In the picture there was this one goofy-looking dude and kids would spend hours trying to find him."

"Yeah," I said, *Where's Waldo!* I remember those. So, does Jon wear red and white stripes too?" I asked.

"Well, it wouldn't surprise me at all," he explained. "He's kind of weird but he's the best producer I've ever met. If you ask him how, he'll tell you the same thing he tells everyone: his key to success is prospecting. That guy works harder on the phones than anyone I've ever seen!"

As we walked into our morning meeting, I scanned the room for the famous Jon Frost. There were three men in the room wearing

50

glasses and I zeroed in on the taller, gray-haired man who best fit the description. He was lanky enough to be considered "Waldo" at a distance but wasn't the dead-ringer I had been expecting, and he didn't seem like a hippy at all.

"Board Call" commenced where each salesperson called out their sales numbers from the previous day in the field, and my anticipation increased as I waited to hear from my new mentor. When it came time to hear from the man with the glasses, his name was written on the whiteboard as "Dale," and I realized he wasn't the man I was looking for after all. I hadn't yet heard from Jon Frost, and I was getting worried that my new mentor had left me in the lurch on my first day.

Salesperson after salesperson reported their numbers and no Jon Frost. At the very end of the meeting, someone spoke from the corner of the room. In a mildly nasal midwestern accent, he reported an incredible day amounting to about $6,000 in commissions. I still couldn't see him but I knew this was the famed Jon Frost. When he stood up at the close of the meeting and approached me, I almost laughed. I could see why he'd been hiding inconspicuously in the corner. Not only did he look like Waldo, he wore a wrinkled suit, an ugly tie, and his curly hair had barely been combed. He introduced himself and I was pretty sure he was nursing a decent-sized hangover. I thought, *How in the world could this be the prospecting guru that everyone in the office aspired to be?*

We made our way back to my desk and he sat down beside me so we could work together. He quickly threw out my company script and scrawled something on a piece of scrap paper. "Say this word for word," he told me. "You might mess it up for a while but, trust me, it works! Just listen to me for a while and then when you're ready, start dialing." He slammed away at the keypad and put the phone on speaker. I was about to watch pure mastery in action.

"Hi, Mrs. White!" he said when his call was answered. "I hope I didn't catch you doing a million things!"

"Busy as always," she replied.

"Good. I'm calling because I'm responsible for getting you the industry-specific information about increasing your local sales income. Did anyone deliver that to you in the past week or so?"

"No, I haven't seen anything," she said. "Who are you with?"

"You probably don't recognize my voice because we haven't met yet. My name is Jon Frost. I actually work for a company called ABC, Inc. You've heard of us, right?"

"Well, no."

"Oh, wow! Well, we specialize in helping businesses to double sales income in a variety of ways. We worked with Taurus, Inc., to train their people and double their profits in seven months. Charaz LLC was on the brink of shutting their doors and now they're back on track after working with us for just three months. What are you currently doing to increase sales at White Enterprises?"

"We hired a marketing consultant a while back and he kind of left us high and dry," she explained. "I've been trying to implement some of the ideas we collaborated on but I'm pretty overwhelmed with all of my other responsibilities."

"What did you enjoy the most when working with the marketing consultant?" Jon asked.

"He was supposed to evaluate the holes in our marketing approach and facilitate the solutions. He left right after he produced a report because he got a big client that demanded his full attention."

"So if you could adjust anything to make things better going forward, what would it be?" Jon prodded.

"I would love it if he could help facilitate these solutions," Mrs. White explained. "They're really good and we believe that they'll work. We just need an expert who can get the ball rolling."

"Mrs. White," Jon asked, "are you the person who makes decisions about the marketing budget for White Enterprises?"

"Yes, I am. The buck stops here," she said proudly.

"So if I could show you some ideas on how to get these solutions you're excited about rolling, you believe your sales will dramatically improve?"

"Absolutely!"

"I'm glad to hear that and there is some great information we should go over together," Jon said. "I'm not sure if we can work together but I'll let you know if there is any way I can help. If you like what you hear, we can move forward, and if not, that's totally okay. I will be near your office early next week, so would Monday or Tuesday work better for you?" I could see Jon getting excited; it was contagious.

"Probably Monday," she answered.

"Perfect, would 1:00 p.m. or 3:00 p.m. work better for your schedule?" he asked.

"Let's do 1:00 p.m."

I couldn't believe my ears. Jon had spent about five minutes on the phone and nailed down an appointment with the first person who'd picked up. After hanging up, he looked at me and gloated, "That's how it's done!"

While it was rare to book a sales appointment on the first call, Jon assured me that his success was due to a simple systematic approach. I found out that Jon had worked at a call center and had sold insurance door to door. During that time, he had learned a simple yet effective way to interact with people no matter what prospecting method he was using. He was confident that his approach would work just as well door to door as it would over the phone. He taught me the simple formula and it has helped hundreds of sales-people enhance their prospecting.

Jon started off by explaining that many rookie salespeople overthink and babble too much to their prospects, making them ineffective. Therefore, it's vital that a system and script facilitate conversation. When rookies prospect, they have a tendency to monopolize the airtime, and the person on the other end is forced to listen to rote recitation. This usually makes the prospect want to hang up and often creates an adversary instead of a client. Jon wanted me to avoid all of that by keeping my prospecting casual! Jon's simple approach worked and I was determined to learn it. He called it CASUAL because he said people are more likely to become clients if we have a casual approach.

The CASUAL Solution

CASUAL was the acronym Jon used when forming his scripts for prospecting. He would make a script for door-to-door, over the phone, or instant messaging / email interactions. The interaction itself didn't matter because it was designed for a single purpose: to facilitate engagement and begin a healthy client relationship. Let's break the acronym apart piece by piece so that you can start using it immediately.

C stands for **Currently**. Jon would attempt to determine what the prospect was currently doing about the problem and how Jon could help him or her to solve it. If he was selling vacuums, Jon would want to know what kind of vacuum his prospect had. If he was selling insurance, he would want to know who they were working with and what coverage they were paying for. "So, who are you currently working with?" he'd always ask.

A stands for **Appreciate**. "What do you appreciate about your current situation?" This was an important question because so many novice salespeople focus on how much better they think they are without taking the time to find out what is important to the prospect. Jon also stressed that we wanted to make sure the new client still got what they currently loved; we only wanted to add to that.

S stands for **Slightly Adjust**. "If you could slightly adjust something to make it better, what would it be?" Because we show that we care about what our client wants, we can further demonstrate our commitment by asking how we can make it better. Lots of salespeople throw benefits against the wall to see what sticks. By simply asking our prospect what they would change to make their life better, we can demonstrate that we care. If we can facilitate the change they wish to see, we're one step closer to making the sale.

U stands for **Understand**. "So, if I'm understanding you right, you like 'x' about your current situation but if 'y' could change, it would make life a lot easier. Is that correct?" Dale Carnegie said the sweetest word to a person's ears is the sound of their own name. I would add that the second sweetest sound is their words repeated back to them, which indicates an understanding of what they said. Summarizing what a prospect has shared with you not only establishes you as an incredible listener; it also helps clear up any miscommunication. This may be the most important step but it's also a result of each proceeding step.

A stands for **Authorized**. "Do you have the authorization to fix this problem?" Jon told me that he learned to ask this the hard way. Early in his career he would sit down with someone and go through the whole sales process only to be told that every decision had to be discussed with someone else. This can be just as aggravating as presenting to a department head only to find out that a CFO needs be part of the decision process but, oh no, he or she is on vacation! Asking this question saves a lot of potential wasted time and energy.

L stands for **Lock Down the Appointment**. The final step in securing a viable client is clearly locking down the appointment. "I've got some ideas that you might like. If you don't, that's fine, but if you do, we can look at moving forward. Would next Monday or Wednesday be better for you to get back together?" You can then zero in on a good time by asking if they'd like to meet in the morning or afternoon. With that you have a focused meeting set with an expected agenda of your sales conversation.

Using this method diffuses the adversarial relationship that so many novice salespeople fear. The method is aptly named CASUAL because that is exactly what it promotes. By aligning ourselves as collaborators with those who might benefit from our offerings, we position ourselves to help. Let's take a CASUAL approach to our prospecting!

Bringing a prospect to the point where they are ready to hear you out takes some finesse. Depending on how you are prospecting, you may want to go forward with the sales process, but there is one more thing we must pay attention to before we move on.

Using the CASUAL technique is very effective but it lacks a transitional piece that Jon learned to automatically incorporate. Just because the prospect feels cared for or understood doesn't automatically mean they want to work with you. People can feel cornered if we assume they want to move forward in the relationship. When I would try moving forward by moving to the next step of the sales process, I would inevitably encounter resistance and would sometimes lose the opportunity. There would be an awkward moment when the prospect resisted and I would feel embarrassed and confused. I was doing everything Jon had taught me but it seemed like I was always falling short. I spent some time listening and taking notes while observing how he worked with his clients and I saw him doing one small thing that seemed to make all the difference.

After he finished walking a client through a CASUAL conversation, Jon always assured them that they were the boss. The client would be in charge of everything going forward. Jon subtly told them they could say no while assuring them that everyone would get along in the end. I couldn't believe I was missing it. It was part of the script Jon had written but I didn't realize how incredibly powerful one little sentence could be.

When you examine the stereotype of salespeople these days, a small step like this makes a lot of sense. People hate the stereotypical pushy salesperson; the word "sales" alone terrifies a lot of people. People often feel that when dealing with a salesperson, they lose autonomy in making decisions.

I am proud to be a sales professional and I feel that a career in sales is one of the most noble choices a person can make. When done ethically, we help people understand why they are frustrated with the status quo and we offer a way to achieve a higher quality of life. It doesn't get much better than that. The only way to fulfill that calling is by doing it ethically and collaborating with people so they too can feel empowered to make the right decision for themselves and their families.

Jon was doing that by making a small but significant statement before he asked for a sale or meeting. "I'm not sure if we will be able to work together, but if you like what I share with you, we can proceed. If not, that's totally okay—we can still be friends!"

Eventually I defined what I learned by creating another acronym, PEP. It worked well because I felt the momentum die if I didn't include that simple element. But adding PEP to the conversation moved things along in the sales relationship. It was just the shot of energy I was looking for.

P: The first P stands for **Possibility**, meaning it's possible that working together might not be the right fit. There is always an element of tension after we walk through the CASUAL technique because people have opened up and become vulnerable. The prospect isn't sure they want to commit to us; they have been conditioned to protect themselves from salespeople. When we say out loud what they are thinking, it lets that tension out and affirms their ability to say no.

E: The E stands for **Empowerment**. It is so important that the prospect feels empowered to make the right decision for him or her. I like to let the prospect know I will share ideas and if they like them, we can proceed together. It hints at the fact that I will share valuable information with them without expecting something in return. I will empower them to make their own decision.

P: The last P stands for **Pals** and it might be the most important. We need to assure the people we are working with that no matter what they decide, we still want to be friends. I have watched inexperienced salespeople burn every bridge imaginable by getting involved in network marketing. They try and leverage relationships to advance their agenda and it blows up in their face. Tell every prospect you speak to that you would rather have a friend than a sale, but more importantly, mean it!

Following a formula is powerful because it allows you as a sales professional to be creative and empowered. No one needs canned corporate script when they can follow proven principles to craft a more effective one on their own. Learning an approach that both eased my prospect's concerns and offered solutions with no strings attached taught me to *love* prospecting. The rookie salespeople driven to quit almost always did so because they hated prospecting. I was bound and determined to find a way to fall in love with what the quitters hated. Turns out, all I needed was a CASUAL approach with a bit of PEP!

CHAPTER 5

Crossing – Introduction (ARCH)

HAVE YOU EVER MET a thickset man who is more squat than chubby? They often have a very round head, a short haircut, and a full chin. I had a boss early in my career who defined the archetype of the "stout man" for me. Because I so closely associated him with the burly impression he made, I remember being surprised when I saw him at the pool during a Cancun incentive trip. I assumed he would have a large gut, but in reality he had the same physique as nearly every other forty-five-year-old man in America. He had a bit of a beer gut (but then, who doesn't?); his average frame somehow enhanced the "hefty" feeling he gave off. This feeling was compounded when he wore a loose black suit. Unbidden, images of bowling balls would come to mind. Despite his looks, he was an important person in my life, as this "little big guy" taught me the value of a first impression.

The story of my old boss demonstrates how memorable first impressions can be. The sage advice "don't judge a book by the cover" is often cited but rarely followed. Each of us has primal instincts that cause us to make snap judgments and assess people when we first meet them, often based on nothing more than physical appearance. There are arguments to be made about the value of snap judgments. Most are based on experience and are designed to limit risk and maximize reward. We've all heard arguments against judging people based on first impressions, but there is also value in doing so.

I learned some great lessons from that old boss but it wasn't always a great experience. While working for him, I found the culture he built to be very toxic. Initially, I had a mixed first impression because, while he was a charming guy, I always felt an underlying sense of gloom when speaking with him. Later, I understood where this feeling was coming from: just beneath the charming façade this man presented to the world, there was an undercurrent of drug use, family problems, and unethical business practices roiling away. Before I knew it, his attitude and the culture he cultivated began to affect me. I started talking down to my wife and kids; I would drink a little too much wine and began to bend the rules if it benefited me. It turned out that my first impression was pretty accurate. Sometimes first impressions are correct. The poet Maya Angelou famously said, "When someone shows you who they are, believe them the first time." In this case, the round man was telling me who he was. I would have saved myself a lot of aggravation if I'd just believed him.

As a result, I learned that I am free to judge constantly—and I encourage you to do the same. Obviously I'm not talking about generalizations based on stereotypes such as racism, sexism, or any of the negative isms; what I really mean is that we should learn to trust our instincts. If we understand how often judgment takes place, we can begin to welcome it instead of fighting it. Unfair and unwarranted judgment is a dirty word, but the kind that helps us to assess a situation and serve people better is not only responsible, it's ethical.

A balance should be established between informed decision making and quick decisions. Both types of decisions are judgments and both typically yield the same verdict. But there is a time to look at all of the details for the sake of wisdom and understanding. Most of the time we need to decide so we can get stuff done.

Let's look into the details of judgment in the context of a familiar experience, grocery shopping. The second I enter the store and see all the choices laid out before me, I begin to judge. I can shop at a trusted corporate store like Safeway, Kroger, or Trader Joe's. I can also shop at the local food co-op or privately owned store. I can even try dumpster diving for perfectly good food that chain stores toss daily. I have lots of options so it's important to weigh them carefully before passing judgment. I'm already exhausted.

In the context of grocery shopping, the fiscally wise approach would be to buy the highest quality food for the lowest price. Dumpster, here we come! There is perfectly safe, consumable food thrown out every day so if we were concerned solely with survival, we would be foolish to let a dumpster opportunity pass. Conversely, the worst decision you could make if finances were your main concern would be too spend as much as possible on your groceries (hello, Whole Foods). Our judgments of others and the world around us often create hardships. But the issue isn't that simple. Imagine dissecting each judgment and decision to determine its total possible impact? That is what's known as analysis to paralysis. We'd spend all our time analyzing every decision that life would pass us by as we stood, frozen with indecision. In order to keep life moving along, we create shortcuts by judging.

When we make a snap judgment, we believe that quality can be assessed by outward appearance. For instance, when I go to Trader Joe's, I see the typical quality I expect from a standard grocery store. I make assumptions about thousands of other products Trader Joe's stocks based on my first impressions and judgments. I see the clientele in trendy yoga pants and North Face down vests and assume that the other shoppers are healthy and confident. Smiling cashiers stand in stark contrast to the depressing atmosphere of other stores. They keep the place clean and offer samples happily. When I rely on my judgment and that judgment tells me that Trader Joe's is worth paying for, I end up staying away from dumpster diving with a guilt-free conscience.

The problem with our judgment shortcuts is that they can be wrong and they can be used against us. That's why people are wary of salespeople; they may be basing their judgment on past experience and trying to protect themselves from an unwanted sales pitch. People with a career in sales need to think about and respect the title "salesperson" much more than they do. I've watched numerous sales hackers feign interest in a prospect only to watch them go down in flames when their agenda rears its ugly head. They were only in it for themselves. Let's not forget that we must earn respect and build relationships if we are to be considered true sales professionals. If you can't wait for people to trust you on their terms, then the sales industry is not for you. But if you embrace the judgment and tell people how much you love sales, you'll go far.

This is why we must to be genuine with our first impression as sales professionals. We must present who we really are. So many salespeople downplay the fact that they are in sales; many use self-deprecating language or even appear embarrassed. People pick up on those self-judgments and will begin to reflect them back at you. Before you know it, it becomes a self-fulfilling prophecy. I believe in a different approach: concise honesty with a large dose of positive attitude. Now that makes for a great first impression!

Third Time's the Charm

Nineteen years ago I began a phase in life with a woman who is the definition of the word "incredible." I am, of course, referring to the dating phase and it didn't come easily. I was a senior in high school at the time and she was a sophomore. She swears she doesn't remember the details but I do.

I fell in love at first sight. Allow me to elaborate a bit. During summer vacation before the beginning of my senior year, I dreamt of a strikingly beautiful woman veiled in white. In my heart, I knew that woman in my dream would be my wife. I had no idea who she was but her face was seared into my mind.

When school began in the fall, my first class of the day was gym. A week or so went by and as I walked into the locker room, I saw the students from the aerobics class lined up waiting to enter the gym. I spotted Jennifer, a friend of mine, sitting on the floor next to a girl I didn't know; I said hello. The girl looked up at me with what I took to be annoyance.[1] I walked on and about five steps later, I froze in front of the locker room door. That girl who had given me the stink eye affected my heart on a primal level. I felt like I'd been hit by a truck. I spun around, and as I went back to find her, I saw that she was making her way into gym class.

---

1 I would later learn that her new gym shoes were killing her feet and the angry look wasn't meant for me!

I would see the same girl at school occasionally but I told myself she only resembled the girl from my dreams; it's what I told myself to feel better because a connection with this girl clearly wasn't happening. I remember sidling up next to her and Jennifer as they walked to the cafeteria. I talked about the band I was in and how great we were but I could tell I wasn't making an impression on my dream girl. At that point, I gave up on trying to annoy her into a conversation and accepted that maybe the woman of my dreams was still out there, somewhere else. What I didn't know was that it was my approach that was all wrong.

Linsey was an office aide responsible for gathering the attendance forms from the classrooms on campus. One afternoon I made my way into the office to speak with my counselor. As I waited for my appointment, my dream girl sat down beside me. She looked right at me and said, "You know what? Guys really suck!"

"Uhhhh," I stammered, "Okay, what do you mean?"

"My date for homecoming just told me he wants to go with his group of guy friends. I already have my dress!" She was fit to be tied.

"Yep," I replied, not knowing what else to say. I wanted to defuse her anger so I kept it vague.

"Yep, what?" she pressed. I felt like she wanted to take her frustration out on me.

"Well, I'm a guy and I totally agree that we all suck!" I said.

She started laughing and it was the sweetest sound I'd ever heard. When she finally stopped, an idea popped into my head. I spent a little time establishing who our mutual friends were and then proposed my solution. "Some of our mutual friends and I are going to homecoming as a group," I said. "I have a really good friend named Britton who would love to go with us but he goes to school across town and in order to come, you need to have a date from our school." I paused, watching for her reaction. "Do you think you would be open to going with all of us so that Britton could come along too?" I asked.

She agreed and we started finding reasons to find each other on campus. After a weird homecoming dance where we both tried to ditch our dates and dance with each other, we had lunch together. As they say, the rest is history! We now have four beautiful children together. Even though it took me three tries to break through, I learned my first valuable sales lesson: focus on their needs.

The Platinum Rule of Sales

Working in sales can be very challenging. The best sales professionals spend most of their time focused on the needs of others. The tricky part is balancing an agenda and personal goals with working to fulfill the needs of the people you are trying to serve.

I was recently coaching a gentleman who didn't want to give up on his sales dreams, but he was finding it difficult to muster the courage to keep trudging forward. I asked him to take me through his sales process, and he sat me down to view a recorded presentation from his corporate marketing team. He found prospects, showed them the video presentation, and asked them if they wanted to buy; that's it. His problem was evident and he confirmed it throughout our conversation. He didn't ask me questions about my family, what I liked about southern Oregon, or what my favorite sport was. He didn't try to make a personal connection. He just wanted to show me his amazing product and claimed that he wanted the "experts" to explain it so it could be done right. He had been taught the Golden Rule of Sales: selling is statistics. He believed that if he showed his presentation to as many people as possible, someone would eventually want what he was offering. I agree with what he was taught, as that's the mantra salespeople have used for over a century, but it comes up short for a sales professional as opposed to a salesperson. A sales professional differentiates himself or herself by enacting a similar but more crucial rule: the Platinum Rule of Sales.

The price of platinum is about 10%–15% higher than gold. Both are precious metals and have great value but there are some differences. Platinum has a much higher melting point than gold; it is also more rare. Platinum can do everything gold can do, but it can do it all better.

When we operate by the Platinum Rule of Sales, we can expect differences in our sales practice. Even though we're only working about 10%–15% harder than with the gold standard, we can do so much more. Platinum can stand up to temperatures double that of what gold can handle. So too, the Platinum Rule of Sales will keep a sales professional from burn out. Platinum is not affected by other compounds the way gold is. Likewise, platinum salespeople can maintain their integrity, while others feel pressure to bend the rules to survive.

Both the Golden Rule of Sales and the Platinum Rule rely on the principle of numbers. The only adjustment has to do with creating slightly more value; the only difference is in the approach we take. Platinum is more valuable than gold, so how do we create more value in a numbers environment? We do it by engaging openly with our prospects, clients, and colleagues.

Selling Is Serving

John Maxwell summarized it perfectly when he said: people don't care how much you know unless they know how much you care. The Golden Rule is for people who like to talk *to* people, while the Platinum Rule is for those who enjoy talking *with* people. For some, serving people is the most exhausting aspect of a career in sales. When we approach people with an eye toward service, we must focus on the needs of others. There is no room for egotistical behavior or self-seeking agendas when we're serving. The only exhausting part of serving is keeping our ego in check! You're familiar with that voice in your head that pushes you to grab for the sale, even if you've only been in sales for a short period of time. That voice reminds you that you have quotas to fill and goals to achieve. It whispers in your ear that you're one of the best and you know all of the tricks to make a prospect buy what you're selling. When I listen to that voice, the funniest thing happens: my prospect starts to sense something. You've probably been on the receiving end of a similar interaction. The other person's words start to become burdensome, obnoxious, and repellant. This is what I like to call commission breath. It's the stench of ego and desperation, and boy, is it gross! Just like the worst case of halitosis, it makes others run for the hills.

As someone who has struggled with commission breath and helped others to overcome it as well, I have developed a few simple principles to counteract that tendency and begin to establish a healthy relationship. This simple step-by-step approach guarantees that you start off on the right foot and focus on the prospect. It gives us the opportunity to share a little about ourselves to establish a personal touch. Finally, we move into establishing credibility for our business and ask for permission to serve our prospects fully. This entry into a great potential relationship is simple to learn. For this approach, we use the acronym ARCH; think of it as a doorway into your new sales method.

An arch is a very old method for building doors and entryways. The Romans used arches in their architecture because they were efficient at sustaining compression stress. An arch will stand the test of time and provides access and egress long after a traditional doorway would crumble. Basing the first impression and introduction of our relationships on an arch will help us to bridge gaps and create bridges with everyone.

The "A" in ARCH Stands for Altruistic

Be Altruistic! Altruism is behavior aimed at helping others. Those who act altruistically are generally unselfish. Every introduction should begin by talking about the other person. Talk about them, show interest in them, focus on them! It is generally acknowledged that people love talking about themselves, so give them an opportunity to do so. I've run an experiment during some of my sales appointments to determine exactly how long someone will talk about him or herself. What I learned is that people can talk anywhere from a few minutes to an hour about themselves before changing the subject! Eventually, most of them would get around to asking me what I was offering; many of them would them sell themselves on the product I presented! I discovered that if I allowed people to talk about themselves for long enough, many of them would run the tank dry! In most cases, my closing ratio would more than double because people love doing business with those they like and almost everyone likes someone who shows interest in them. I made a commitment to only make offers to people I liked. As a result, I spent lots of time trying to become friends with people before they became clients. Of course, there were always people who were negative and pessimistic and couldn't avoid gossip, so I would thank them for their time and find other more positive people with whom to do business. As long as I remembered to look out for the well-being of others, I was golden . . . or better yet, platinum!

The "R" Stands for Relatable

When most people talk about themselves, they will eventually tire of the sound of their own voice. When they are done talking, it becomes your turn. But don't make the mistake of airing your dirty laundry or peddling your product or service. Talk a little bit about yourself and make it personal, but always bring it back to how it relates to them. Keep the focus on what you have in common. This shows that you care and can relate to a prospect on a personal level. It shows that you've been listening.

When my wife and I really connect with another couple, it's usually because we've been able to volley the conversation back and forth. This happens when you listen, relate, and ask follow-up questions. It's super fun, no one gets left out, and everyone feels valued. If we're successful relating to our prospects, we'll be successful in the next step as well.

The "C" Stands for Credible

By establishing yourself and your company as a credible option for your prospect to consider, you approach them with class. The salesperson that is overly excited about attempting to sell a product often fails to understand that not everyone needs what they're offering. If we take time to establish our position as a professional working for a trustworthy company, we bring value to the interaction. Even if a business opportunity does not arise this time, we lay the groundwork for future possibilities.

The "H" stands for Helpful

The final element in a world-class introduction is when we ask for permission to be helpful. By asking permission we are bringing our introductions to the next level. So many people are used to being overwhelmed with information that promises to be life changing, but very little of that information actually delivers on the promises. When we approach people with humility and we ask them permission to help, it affirms their importance. When customers and clients work with a professional who operates on these principles, they know special things are in store.

Putting It All Together

The ARCH principle is an excellent theory but seeing it in action is truly transformative. Consider the following conversation and envision the way you might use it in your own business:

> **Me**: Hi, I haven't met you yet; my name is Erik. Tell me your name!
>
> **Prospect**: I'm David. Good to meet you.
>
> **Me**: One of my best friends is named David! So great seeing you here today. So, tell me, how long have you lived in the area?

(I ask this question because it is inoffensive, generic, and almost always leads to a question like, "Where's your favorite place to go to dinner?")

The Altruistic conversation will continue, focusing on the prospect and allowing them to talk about themselves. Eventually, he or she will ask a question about me. At this point, I've learned enough to say something about myself that's relatable to the prospect, such as the following:

> **Me**: I grew up in the area and met my wife in high school here. My four kids go to the local elementary school, and I work for Pro Sales Consulting. You've heard of Pro Sales Consulting, right?
>
> *(I keep my personal information brief to support the credibility of my company.)*
>
> **Prospect**: No, I haven't heard of that company.
>
> **Me**: Oh! Pro Sales Consulting focuses on doubling sales income in 365 days by focusing on three areas: process/Skills, self-management, and beliefs. What I do is ask a few questions to see if I might be able to help. If I can I will let you know and if not, we can still be friends. Sound good?
>
> *(After establishing credibility by communicating the use of a proven process, I ask permission to see if I might be able to help.)*

In the end, most people will want to move forward and share their frustrations, pains, and obstacles. Some won't and that is totally okay. This approach allows for an organic sales conversation to occur that may not otherwise have happened. If you're tired of ineffective networking, try this approach. Create a script from these principles and bring in your own personal details. You'll be surprised with the response you get!

CHAPTER 6

Fitness – Needs Analysis (FIT)

O N A CRISP AUTUMN DAY, an elderly New Yorker was walking north on Seventh Avenue to grab lunch. Fall in New York is an incredible time of year, and as he made his way up Seventh Avenue he caught glimpses of Central Park between breaks in traffic. The trees were turning color quickly, as the nights were getting progressively colder. It was the perfect afternoon to enjoy a warm lunch.

The man had decided on matzo ball soup from his favorite deli. He had beaten the lunch rush and made his way into the restaurant. He approached the host station past the buzzing lights of the display case where mile-high pies spun under twinkling lights. He heard plate after plate of massive sandwiches slam onto the line. The wait staff yelled their frustrations at the cooks and were rewarded with shakes of the cooks' heads. At this deli, the great food was only half of the experience.

The old man was seated, surrounded by black-and-white photos signed by celebrities and dignitaries. The server stopped at his table, a flip notebook in hand. With rushed kindness he asked, "What will it be, sir?"

"A matzo ball soup, please!" the man said, beaming from ear to ear.

"Excellent choice! Anything else sir?"

"Not at this time, young man, but thank you. Just the soup."

The server was already gone. It didn't take long for the soup to arrive. When the bowl was set down it sent billowy steam into the air; the smell was amazing. It was too hot to eat right away so the man spent a few minutes watching other patrons enjoy lunch while he waited for his soup to cool.

After a few moments, the server noticed that the man had not yet begun to eat. He wasn't surprised because the soup always came off the line practically boiling but plenty of time had passed for the soup to cool. Noticing that the man was waiting an abnormally long time, he stopped by to check on his patron.

"Sir, I noticed you haven't started on your soup yet. Did the soup burn your mouth? It's always so hot when it comes out of the kitchen."

The older man looked up and offered, "Taste the soup!"

"I'm sorry, sir, is the flavor off? We have a new cook back there and there have been a few problems already today. I'll take it back."

The old man put his hand up to stop the young server and said emphatically, "Taste the soup."

"Sir, I think I understand. There is a fly in the soup, isn't there? They seem to come out in droves every fall. Let me get you a new bowl right away!" The server turned red with embarrassment.

The old man slammed his hand on the table, looked the young server in the eye, and said, "Please stop! Just taste the soup!"

The young server was exasperated. He decided to indulge the old man. Looking all over the table he angrily asked, "Okay, I'll try your soup, but where is the friggin' spoon?"

"Aha!" the old man wagged his finger in the air.

Stunned, the server replied sheepishly, "So sorry, sir. I will be right back with your soup spoon!"

All too often we find ourselves in a predicament where we believe we know the best way to serve a client. Experience in sales can work against some of the sharpest salespeople because we have a tendency to jump to conclusions regarding what we think a prospect needs. The story above illustrates the importance of finding out what the client needs without assuming we know.

Have you ever presented the benefits of a product or service to a prospect with a glazed look on his or her face? Have you ever asked for the sale and had the prospect tell you they don't see how it can help? Some salespeople will close a sale over and over while ruining the relationship and setting themselves up for a future cancellation. These frustrations are a result of a poor needs analysis. If a needs analysis isn't done properly, the sales cycle grinds to a halt.

Think of all the people who have been coerced into buying something they didn't need. What do they usually say about the salesperson who talked them into it? "They were pushy!" It blows my mind how beginner salespeople fear being pushy yet they consistently push their prospects to buy because they aren't willing to ask a few questions. Most beginners feel they are losing control of the sale when they start asking questions. Instead they focus on telling prospects what's best for them. Distance begins to form when a salesperson speaks more than he or she listens. Sometimes a prospect will even totally disengage. The novice salesperson beats prospects over the head with benefits and talks right past the sale, wearing him or herself out in the process. "Sales is hard work!" they say, but without a needs analysis they're just making it harder on themselves.

Never Tell What You Can Ask

In sales, need is the name of the game. Every product or service fills a need or solves a problem. Some solutions are universal, while others solve specific or rare problems. Many prospects have needs that have caused them pain for years; there are even more people who don't know they need a solution because they are unaware that they even have a problem. Everyone and every business in the world has problems; salespeople have the incredible opportunity to help solve those problems.

In the last chapter we learned how to use our introduction to prepare our prospect to answer some quick questions. We want to ask questions to determine if what we offer is the right fit for our prospects. We even let the prospect know that it's okay if we can't work together, but furthering the discussion through questions is the only way to determine that. If the prospect agrees to proceed, you're set to start asking.

When I was nineteen years old, I learned how to weld from a man who didn't know he was teaching me; his name was Mike. Mike was raised in Florida, where he learned how to weld, but he left to follow large construction companies building huge projects all over the United States. He ended up in Alaska, where he took a welding job on the oil pipeline. The job lasted for so long that Mike found a house and settled down for a while in Alaska, about as far away from his home state of Florida as he could get. Mike called himself "the southerner from the North." Pipeline work slowed, forcing Mike back on the road to find additional work. I met Mike in upstate New York, where he was working on a huge construction project. He liked me and we began having lunch together every day.

I had always wanted to learn how to weld but I thought I would have to go to school for it. When I met Mike, I wanted him to teach me but was too afraid to ask. I was working on a project at home and I needed a bolt welded to a steel plate, so I brought it into work one day knowing Mike would do it for me.

"Hey, Erik," Mike said when I called him. "I'm really busy today so just stop by the welding shop and you can weld your own stuff. Jerry's out sick today." Jerry was the welder who worked right next to Mike; occasionally they shared tools. I didn't know what to say so I froze. Mike thought I knew how to weld, and telling him I didn't suddenly seemed humiliating.

"Erik, did you hear me?" he asked.

"Yeah," I said. "Are you sure that's allowed?" I tried to defer to the rules, hoping to take the pressure off me.

"I don't see why not. You can weld, right?" he asked.

"Come on!" I said, laughing nervously. "You know they taught a monkey how to weld, right?" I don't know why I responded in such an ambiguous way; I think I was just embarrassed about my lack of skill. Whatever the reason, I learned the power of asking the right questions.

As we made our way to the welding shop, my heart was beating like I had just sprinted a mile. I laid the parts on the table and stared at them. In a moment of panic, an idea flashed in mind. "Mike," I said, "can you walk me through the setup on this welder? I've never worked with one like this."

"Sure!" he said. He showed me where to adjust the amperage and set it to the appropriate setting for what I was welding. He walked through the safety checklist and made sure I had the right welding helmet. He noticed Jerry was running low on welding rods.

"With that amperage what rods would you use?" I asked.

"Probably some 6013 rods. You don't want to melt through that plate," he said. "Hey, if it's been a while you might want to practice on some scrap so you don't foul up your parts."

Gloved and hooded, I brought the electrode down on some scrap steel; the electric arc flashed through the cobalt viewing glass in the welding hood.

"You're moving too fast," I heard Mike say from behind me. I slowed down and the electrode stuck to the scrap steel plate. I pried the electrode off the steel and practiced again. I started getting into the rhythm.

"Hey, nice little pile of dimes buddy!" Mike said. It felt great to hear him cheering me on. I took the welding hood off and chipped the slag away. The weld looked horrible but I had come a long way just by asking the right questions. I practiced the rest of the day and found "projects" to weld all over my garage. Eventually I got pretty good. I've even made some money by welding for friends!

One day I told Mike that he taught me to weld. We had a long laugh together about that because he had thought that something seemed a bit off. He was under the impression that it had been so long I had forgotten all of the basics. He didn't think it was my very first welding experience. He was just glad I hadn't burned the welding shop down!

That experience taught me that you can get very far by asking the right questions. If I had told Mike that I didn't know how to weld, he would have welded my project for me and I would never have learned how to weld for myself. When we ask questions, we uncover possibilities that would otherwise pass us by.

Just Collaborate and Listen

No one likes to listen to a salesperson go on and on about how terrible life is without the product or service your offer. When we enter into a sales conversation with a prospect there are many reasons they already feel vulnerable. The prospect innately thinks salespeople are trying to get them to buy something; this causes adversarial feelings before the conversation begins. Many people have these feelings because they've experienced unethical pressure tactics in the past. The lecturing approach can also be demeaning because many prospects remember an authority figure from their past saying something like "Because I said so!" As adults, we guard our autonomy fiercely, so it is vital for us to approach a prospect's decision with respect by using an approach that relies on collaboration.

Asking lots of questions facilitates a collaborative environment. Sales professionals don't want to spend a lot of time talking because time spent listening to a prospective client is far more valuable. After all, we want our product or service to solve the problems they actually have, not the ones we *think* they might have.

Rookies spend a lot of time trying to force sales on prospects based on a perceived need. These rookies typically get very frustrated and claim that asking questions doesn't work. They often feel that the meeting is getting away from them and would rather cut their losses and avoid questions altogether. They feel that by asking fewer questions and having shorter meetings, they can hold more meetings and, as a result, close more sales. I can understand this perspective when questioning seems ineffective, so I will often ask these rookies what types of questions they're asking.

"Have you ever used _____ before?" is what I usually hear first. Other times I hear, "Do you want to improve your facility production?" Rookies love to say they are "building their yeses," which means they're trying to get the prospect in the habit of saying "yes" so that when the close comes, they will walk mindlessly into the sale. But I think the person "building their yeses" is trying to make an infomercial. Don't most infomercials start that way?

"Do you get frustrated with food sticking to the pan?"

"Do you hate it when you can't flip a pancake?"

"Does it make you mad seeing the Teflon in your food?"

"Then act now . . ."

Novice salespeople start off with this approach because it's what they know or it's worked for them in the past. This approach relies heavily on closed questions, questions with yes or no answers. Closed questions can be useful in certain scenarios but they should not be used heavily in the needs analysis component of the sales cycle. In the needs analysis, our goal is uncovering, examining, and determining if a problem exists. To do that, sales professionals must use open questions.

Open questions are great; I love them. They are helpful in sales, relationships, financial discussions, self-talk, or even when learning how to weld! Open questions can't be answered with a yes or no. Instead, they're more like the following:

"Tell me your thoughts regarding . . ."

"How would you feel if . . .?"

"On a scale of one to ten, where are you now? Why?"

"Why?"

"What would happen if . . . ?"

Open questions promote collaboration and discussion. When you ask an open question, it gives the prospect an opportunity to take the sales conversation in their preferred direction. It can feel a little like losing control but that's the way it's supposed to feel. A sales professional should function like a doctor helping a patient feel comfortable. There is vulnerability in a relationship; trust is developed with each question. Patients and prospects both need to feel free of judgment when sharing painful issues to which they're looking for solutions. Open questions facilitate teamwork and prepare the relationship for future collaboration. Let's face it: it's hard to ask for help and people love to feel self-sufficient. When you ask open questions, prospects can feel like they took part in the solution instead of just throwing money at a problem.

What Are You Looking For?

"I need to get an idea of your range of motion and understand how to help you. Just let me know on a one-to-ten scale where your pain is."

I started wondering what I had gotten myself into. A coworker of mine had referred me to his chiropractor. I had been hesitant to go because I had heard horror stories of people leaving chiropractors' offices broken and in pain. But I had been experiencing excruciating neck pain and I could only turn my head a few degrees in either direction. Something was misaligned and I needed it fixed, but I didn't want bones popped and cracked! I was feeling desperate.

"So let me get this straight," I asked. "You're going to cause pain to find pain?"

"Yes and no," the chiropractor explained. "I need to see your range of motion in other parts of your body. Stresses in other spots could be creating most of the pain you're experiencing in your neck.

Some of those other places might need adjustment to relieve the pain you're feeling. Think of a crack in a two-by-four," he explained. "Chances are that the board was experiencing stress in other places and the damage has manifested in the weakest spot."

"Alright, alright," I said. "Do what you need to do."

He poked and prodded, stretched and pushed. A little later I was able to move my neck and I also had a better range of motion in general. There were some painful moments but after his explanation I had accepted that I had to go through the pain to get the relief. Finding the pain is the key to solving problems.

Finding pain should be our number one priority when we conduct a needs analysis within our sales cycle. Salespeople won't be poking and prodding people to find the pain; open questions are the tools we need to use. We can follow a very simple principled approach that facilitates open questions while determining if what we offer is a good fit.

Is It a Good FIT?

The needs analysis is upheld by the FIT principle. The acronym works very well because we are trying to help the prospect determine if working with us is a good fit.

F: Find the pain.

The first step in the FIT process is finding the pain. This can be the most daunting part of the process. Open questions can lead many different places, but finding the pain will be easier than you think. Imagine you're meeting with a CEO concerned with performance consulting. You might start out by asking, "What do you feel would impact overall production the most?" or "How have you motivated your people to do something they didn't think was possible?" If you find yourself chatting with someone about nutritional supplements a good question would be, "Tell me about your experience taking supplements in the past," or "What good and or bad things did you experience?" If you are an insurance agent, you might ask, "What coverage have you needed in the past?" or "Why were they important?" Think about what you have to offer and ask a question that opens a conversation about your industry. You can follow that up by asking what was great, what wasn't so great, what they missed about it, and what they learned. All of the information you gather is exactly what you need to offer something later. The best part is that by answering the questions, the prospect tells you how they *must* be sold.

I: Intensify the pain.

Motivating through rewards is overrated. I used to think that I was motivated by rewards but I realized that I was actually being motivated by the fear of experiencing pain. I was in a team-based sales contest where top producers and struggling producers were mixed. The prizes were pretty great so I thought I was vying for cool electronics and expensive dinners until I looked at the leaderboard one morning. My team was neck and neck with the most unethical top producer in the whole region. I started working twice as hard after the fear of losing to the charlatan of my office become a possibility. My team ended up winning the contest, but the real payoff for me was not seeing my fears materialize.

Pain and avoiding pain are what really drive decisions. It is critical to a sales professional that the pain a prospect feels be intensified. This seems horrible at first glance but if we find pain in the first step and a prospect never thinks about how things will get worse in the future, they won't be ready to make a change. A personal trainer might first ask, "What kind of physique would you like to have?" and intensify the pain by asking, "How long have you wanted a physique like that?" Finally, he or she will ask, "If you don't do something about it soon, what will that do to your emotional health?" A realtor might start off with "Tell me how your dream home differs from where you currently live" and follow up with "How would you feel if you found out that your dream home is out there right now and someone else is putting an offer in on it next week?"

Intensifying the pain is a necessary step to making the prospect realize that they do, in fact, need what you're offering. They've already told you they need your help; now you're making them understand just how much.

T: Treat the pain.

After we've found a prospect's pain and intensified it, we can treat it. This is the best part of the needs analysis. It also completes about 80% of the sale. Using a simple summary is the best way to treat a client's pain. Here are a few examples:

- "So, if I'm hearing you right, you would like to come up with an employee incentive plan because it worked so well in the past, but you'd like to implement it in the fourth quarter for budgeting reasons. Did I get that right?"

- "I'm hearing that certain supplements have upset your stomach in the past but you know that they're vital to your future health. If there was something that helped you feel great now and didn't upset your stomach, would you be interested in hearing about it?"

By treating the pain we've uncovered and intensified, we are preparing the prospect for the next step in the sales process: the presentation. The presentation is customized and suited to the prospect's needs because we have already discovered the pain together. Everyone hates being in pain and most prospects are ready to buy if we give them a good enough reason.

Start using FIT immediately to transform your sales approach. Connect with people and be a problem solver. Try this Hater exercise:

"I hate having to plan vacation!"

"I hate paying for _____!"

"I hate having to _____!"

There is a lot of pain behind the statement "I hate . . ." By brainstorming how your product or service can take away that pain, you will develop great questions to ask a prospect when trying to find pain.

CHAPTER 7

Pacesetting - Presentation

O N APRIL 22, more than 192 countries across the globe celebrate Earth Day. The holiday is held to celebrate and demonstrate support for environmental protection. Today Earth Day is focused on climate protection, sustainable resources, reduce/reuse/recycle efforts, and the promotion of clean energy.

Growing up in the 1980s, I rarely took notice of Earth Day. In no way was I opposed to the idea of the holiday; I had just never been taught the finer points of a celebration of the planet. When April 22 came around teachers would put in a VHS tape of the Captain Planet superhero cartoon show and the class would collectively roll their eyes. My peers and I cared about the environment but the way environmentalists presented their views to us was, at best, ineffective.

One can always rely on Hollywood to bring an issue front and center for the American people. In 2004, the movie *The Day after Tomorrow* was released, opening minds to the possibility of a modern ice age. The movie didn't win any Oscars and was scoffed at by real scientists but it created questions in the minds of many average moviegoers. The questions were hypothetical but huge implications existed right below the surface. While *The Day after Tomorrow* focused on the absurd and sensational, real science with dire predictions had been televised on the evening news for years yet produced no significant impact. Hollywood seemed better at moving people, even if fact and truth weren't the priorities. The stage was set for one of the greatest presentations in modern time regarding climate change.

The same day *The Day after Tomorrow* was released, Laurie David saw Al Gore's presentation on climate change and was convinced it must be made into a full-length documentary. In his presentation, Gore outlined the dire state of the planet due to our uninhibited emission of greenhouse gasses. He went on to illustrate the impact that melting polar ice would have on coastal cities due to climate change. Real science was presented but painful implications were the focus of the presentation. Viewers left the presentation burdened by the science and intent on making a change.

Two years later, the documentary version of Al Gore's slide show on climate change was released. *An Inconvenient Truth* was met by American audiences with critical acclaim. The film went on to earn an Oscar for Best Documentary, eventually leading to the Nobel Peace Prize for Al Gore. With the release of the documentary, a groundswell of support for legislation reducing greenhouse gases and corrective action to reverse the damage mankind had wrought on the environment moved into overdrive. While legislation around climate change is fiercely debated, Gore's approach in presenting a case is a landmark triumph. No matter what side of the issue you fall on, it is universally accepted that Al Gore's presentation worked; there is no denying that.

In 2006, many were aware of Earth Day but the vast majority of people understood very little about the causes it was built on. But if you asked the same group about *An Inconvenient Truth*, you'd have a hard time finding someone who wasn't familiar with the film and its message. For thirty-six years there had been a globally recognized day focused on protecting the climate, but it had gone largely unnoticed by the majority of the population. In 2006, with the release of *An Inconvenient Truth*, millions of people became advocates for the environment seemingly overnight. For the first time, politically opposed nations began to rally around reversing the climate devastation that threatens everyone globally. This same presentation that has uncovered new sympathizers has also been instrumental in galvanizing opposing views. Why did *An Inconvenient Truth* cause such a shift in our global advocacy for protection of our climate? How did Mr. Gore present the information is such a way that the listener was free to decide where to stand on the issue? To understand how to create an impact that changes behavior, we need to dig a little deeper.

Are We There Yet?

In preparation for making an offer through an effective presentation, we use the FIT technique in our needs analysis. We work to uncover hidden pain a prospect is experiencing. All of the FIT questions should be directed toward a solution that we offer. That should go without saying, but there are many talkative salespeople out there who ask questions that end up painting them into a corner. Beginner sales interviews can start off with some great open questions and then, about three questions deep, the sale gets away and that sales-person finds him or herself lost and without an idea about where to take the meeting.

My youngest son, Matthew, makes this type of mistake all the time in a different context. Matthew is passionate and likes to experience life at one hundred miles per hour. Matt is the baby of the family and was born in the car on the way to the hospital, the circumstances of his birth seeming to set the tone for his life thus far. He wants to arrive at his destination and goes full throttle the whole way, never considering the consequences. Inevitably, he shoots out ahead of everyone else and looks around wondering where the rest of the family is. You've probably seen people like us in the super-market parking lot. We are the family that causes you to slam on your brakes because our lone Matthew is running full tilt to grab a grocery cart. We almost had to shut down part of Disneyland when Matthew decided he had to get in line for Buzz Lightyear Astro Blasters as the park was closing.

From a parental perspective, Matthew's energy can be over-whelming but it comes from an innocent place. Many salespeople experience the same thing when they start to try to understand a prospect's pain and find a possible solution. We can all be a little hasty when we get excited about the sales process; then we start rushing ahead. Seeing a possible sale, we rush forward only to look behind and find that our prospect has been left in the dust. By adjusting our approach, we can really start to help people and generate some sales at the same time.

By learning from Al Gore's approach to presenting climate change, we can get some great points that help presenters, salespeople, and even my rambunctious youngster! Gore had been presenting his lecture to hundreds of audiences all over the globe. As a result, he has been honing his effective presentation techniques for years. Gore developed discipline and confidence, which gave him the ability to dramatically affect the thoughts and actions of the audience at his presentations. He began with passion, which pushed him onto the stage in spite of his humiliation as a failed presidential hopeful. Over and over, that passion drove him to refine his message for his audience. His ability to connect with humility allowed his presentation to gain unstoppable momentum. He'd discovered that presenting with impact involves passion mixed with discipline and humility.

How do you teach a second grader to mix passion with discipline? Trust me, it is no small feat! The passion of an eight-year-old is impossible to control completely, so instead we take the approach of helping Matt see the value in self-discipline. When we start out in a sales career we all need a little reining in. The challenge can be learning how to self-direct that kind of discipline. We focus on a few principles with Matthew that translate very well when salespeople struggle with runaway sales and developing self-discipline.

1. **Learn to enjoy the journey.** When Matthew bolts away, he is usually trying to get to the same place we're all headed. Matthew sees value in the goal instead of the process. All of my children focus on the destination from time to time. "Are we there yet?" is a common question when we travel. Linsey and I have gotten creative and work to help our children find value in the journey. We blast some great music to sing along to, play a car game, or find something fun to experience along the way. A great approach to enjoying the sales "journey" is to tell yourself how much you love

asking questions, making friends, and finding perfect clients with whom to work. If you don't love those things yet, don't worry. Anyone can learn to love them; free yourself to start having fun along the way and you won't regret it!

2. **Learn to match their pace.** Matthew never thinks he is going too fast; he believes the rest of the world is going too slow. It might be difficult to slow things down because of how you envision the sale but it is important to understand that prospects don't always share the same vision. Instead, we should wait for cues that signal when it's the right time to transition. A prospect will usually ask about you when they get tired of talking about themselves; that's your cue to share information about yourself. As you conduct your needs analysis you might hear, "That's a really good question," or "I hadn't thought about that before." When you generate responses like that, you know you're getting ready to transition into a presentation.

3. **Probably most important is to remember to focus on the relationship.** We spend a lot of time learning about our children. When they run off ahead of us or get impatient with our long journeys we miss out on who they are because we're concerned with managing them. Kids and adults alike need training in how to immerse themselves in the moment. Being genuine in your relationships will translate into sales. Transitioning from a mindset that focuses on sales to one that responds to relationships will unlock unknown abilities.

This approach to self-discipline is dramatically different than most of what you will hear from self-discipline experts. We are used to hearing, "Grind it out!" "Forge ahead," and "Fight your way through." Those motivational exclamations are helpful and necessary but only in the right context. Motivational prodding is effective when we use it on ourselves but it tends to be more effective with others if we use a light touch. Stephen Covey's advice reigns supreme: "With people, fast is slow and slow is fast." The discipline in relationships and decision making focuses on serving others, so if we rush that, people can feel marginalized.

Overload

One of my favorite quotes is "The brain can absorb only as much as the seat can endure." I have been guilty of ignoring this truth but it always ends the same way: in no sales. Getting a handle on how much information we give a prospect is an art. Knowing how much information someone needs to make a decision is tricky. I have found that giving too much information is far worse than leaving some details out.

Recently I was talking with someone who was new to the world of sales. She was very passionate about her product yet had no idea what I did. Her first mistake was not making an effort to learn anything about me. She started going on and on about how amazing her product was and I listened politely. Next she delved into the statistics and scientific facts and I soon found my mind wandering. I was fixated on how many mistakes she was making instead of listening to her presentation. She droned on and as she got to the point in her presentation where she asked for my interest, I refocused. "I'm not sure," I said. "I need more information." Most of us are conditioned to respond that way when we aren't ready to make a decision. She gave me a ton of printed material on her product and I found the nearest trash can.

Even if this novice product peddler had handled things differently, the result was probably going to be the same. She may have approached me with relationship creation in mind and asked me questions to generate some pain, but the information overload would still have been her downfall. She had worked as a scientific researcher and knew a lot about how her product worked; therefore, she felt it was her duty to educate everyone so that they could take action. She genuinely believed that she could change lives by sharing the news. The only problem with the message was its length. She had facts, figures, pamphlets, CDs, websites, video testimonies, and newsletters but no sales.

According to psychologist Lucy Jo Palladino, Ph.D., "Information overload occurs when a person is exposed to more information than the brain can process at one time."[2] When we encourage someone to make a decision about our product or service and we then tell them everything we know, people are often repelled. Palladino confirms this by saying, "When you're overwhelmed by too many choices, your brain mildly freezes and by default you passively wait and see." We experience this paralysis analysis because subconsciously we don't want to make a bad decision, so we put things on hold.

Novice salespeople see this hesitation and interpret it to mean that they aren't giving enough information so they flood their prospect with more useless sales fodder. Prospects start running for the hills when they sense a fire hose of information coming their way. The saddest part is how quickly a relationship between a sales-

---

2 *Find Your Focus Zone: An Effective New Plan to Defeat Distraction and Overload* (New York: Free Press, 2007).

person and their product can be ruined by unbridled sales passion. The salesperson grows bitter toward the product/service/company they were championing and scoffs at others who are successful when in fact the problem was closer to home.

I have been known to leave details out in my presentations. I've never had a client sign a check until they get the answers they were looking for—it just doesn't happen. If I try to answer all the questions I think they might have, the deal falls apart. Most of the people I have overinformed don't want to talk to me again. I assume they think there was something fishy about my offer because I had to go over so many details. I get the same feeling when I sign a long legal document. Every time I sign a contract like that I wonder if I signed away my firstborn. It's possible to drown in details.

Balance

In the film *Karate Kid*, Daniel LaRusso learns the basics of karate from his elderly mentor, Mr. Miyagi. One of the most important lessons Daniel learns is balance. On a sunny afternoon, Daniel and Mr. Miyagi go the beach to train and Mr. Miyagi sends Daniel into the ocean to battle the waves and learn balance. The water rushes up and pulls at Daniel's feet while waves crash down around him. There is a learning curve for anyone who wades out into the ocean because there are dangerous forces that have taken the lives of even experienced swimmers. By developing his ability to balance, Daniel hones the skills, which eventually allows him to defeat his rival in the championship fight.

There is a lot to be said for balance. Our ability to present solutions in a balanced way will lead to more sales and recurring business in the future. A balanced approach builds trust and fosters a sense of camaraderie. Prospects learn to enjoy the sales process and many end up excited about buying.

How can we achieve this powerful balance? Sales professionals craft balanced presentations by focusing on between one and three of the painful problems discovered in the needs analysis. Instead of spending extra time plunging the depths of prospect pain and running the risk of wearing down your prospects, focus instead on between one and three pain points. With a small number of painful problems that can be treated, most people will sacrifice the money to fix the problem. This leaves the door open to more buying experiences in the future.

The Last Five Minutes

Every basketball game I have ever watched can be summarized by the last five minutes. For most of the game, teams trade points back and forth. The last quarter is always the most important and most games are decided in the last minute if not the last few seconds. A sales presentation begins the last quarter of the game.

When the presentation begins, the prospect should be keenly aware of the problem they have. If the needs analysis was done properly, they will make sacrifices to solve their problem and alleviate their pain. All you have to do is know your product well enough to highlight the appropriate features and explain how those features will translate to benefits. Basically, you're playing smart for the last quarter. Avoid mistakes and direct the prospect where you want him or her to go.

CHAPTER 8

Milestones - Closing

WHEN YOU DON'T KNOW what to do, you do only what you know. I wanted to close more clients and was reading lots of books about closing but I still couldn't find the magic, the right blend of skills and know-how that would allow me to close. One day, after reading for hours I decided to mix it up a bit. I had heard about some films about salespeople and decided to come at the topic of closing from a different angle. I got a list of "sales cinema" and started with a film I had never heard of, *Glengarry Glen Ross*.

I wanted to familiarize myself with the film a little so I did some quick background research. I learned that it was originally a play in 1984 and had won a Pulitzer Prize. In 1985, Joe Mantegna received a Tony award for his portrayal of Ricky Roma in the play. Al Pacino was nominated for an Academy Award and a Golden Globe for his performance of the same character in the 1992 film adaptation.

After seeing these accolades, I figured I had found the perfect film to teach me how to close a sale.

In the movie, Alec Baldwin plays Blake, a no-nonsense trainer from the main office come to lay down the law. His performance is both one of the shortest and the most jarring of the film. He berates and humiliates the struggling office of salesmen and dangles their jobs in front of them. Drawing a line in the sand, he makes it clear that most of them will be fired and only the top two salesman will be allowed to keep their jobs. His training meeting climaxes with his "ABC" lesson: "A—always. B—be. C—closing. Always. Be. Closing!" He strides from desk to desk leaning over to breathe insults into the faces of the broken salesmen. He locks eyes with each of them in a primal staring contest that crushes their spirits one at a time as they sheepishly avert their eyes from the Alpha. The scene leaves the viewer feeling anxious, fearful, desperate, and embarrassed for the broken salesmen. We know that these men have to start closing some serious business, and fast.

Instead of motivation and encouragement, the results of the so-called "sales strategy meeting" are defeat and dread. The rest of the film is filled with desperation and tragedy as the salesmen pressure everyone around them into signing on "the line that is dotted" in hopes of saving their jobs. The culture that erupts from the pressure to close at all costs tears the office apart. In the end, a career in sales looks very scary. The model of a good closer is an unethical ravenous dog who looks to kill or be killed. To put it mildly, it wasn't exactly the advice I was looking for.

I didn't learn how to close a sale from *Glengarry Glen Ross,* but I did learn something about closing. A scene at the end of the movie between the office manager, Mr. Williamson, played by Kevin Spacey, and Ricky Roma provided me with the hidden truth I was looking for. In the scene, Mr. Williamson has ruined Roma's sale, which was hanging by a thread. He did so by interrupting Roma's sales conversation to assure the wavering client that his check had been cashed already, causing the client to completely back out of the deal. The failed deal cost Roma $6,000 in commission and a new car. At the end of Roma's very long tirade focusing on Mr. Williamson's inexperience and uselessness, he says, "You never open your mouth without knowing the shot." Experience had taught Roma to always know the answer before asking the question. He had learned that there was a cycle to a sale and when things were out of order, they crumble fast. The message in that scene is that closing is more of a result than a skill.

Perception

Glengarry Glen Ross and many other films that glorify aggressive sales tactics elevate closing as the most important skill available to a salesperson. There is a perception that closers are the snipers of the sales force. People wrongly assume that closers make the most commission, as if by magic. Struggling salespeople beg closers to teach them the "tricks" and ask them to help on tough cases, believing that the mere presence of a closer can tip the deal in their favor.

The false perception of a closer's superpowers exists because many salespeople are lazy or untrained. They think they need a hero to save the sale. Just as a baseball team can call in a closer to preserve a one-run lead in the late innings, many salespeople believe they cannot close the deal themselves and need a specialist to perform the task. Often when someone fails at something and sees someone else do it with ease, they believe the other person must have superhuman skill. Rather than acknowledge that we may not be good at something because we haven't practiced it or put in the time to develop the skills, we assume the other person is naturally gifted. Watching someone bench-press five hundred pounds can seem superhuman too, but if we think about it for a moment we'll realize that they didn't come out of the womb doing it. There were decades of commitment to training, learning, and failing that led to that ability. It's the same in sales.

You may have picked up this book to hone your closing skills and become a superhuman closer. If that's the case, I have some bad news for you: after you finish this book, you probably still won't be the Captain America of Sales. Being a top closer takes commitment to all the things we have touched on so far. You wouldn't expect someone to compete at the Olympic level after simply reading about the sport. Practice, repetition, and the development of habits are needed. Closers are made the same way.

Reality

When I lived in Colorado, I was helping to fix the retirement savings of a retired ski school instructor named Butch who lived in the mountains. His wife had passed away years before and he was concerned about the returns he was getting on his nest egg. As I sat on a dilapidated couch in his manufactured home, I learned that he had over $5 million in the bank earning next to nothing in interest. It was early in my career and finding a prospect with that much money made me excited and overwhelmed at the same time. We brainstormed some ideas that he responded to well and I told him I would get back to him soon.

When I got back to the office I raced into my sales manager's office with the news. I felt like I was in way over my head and I knew that my sales manager had been an incredible closer in his heyday. I was hoping he would join the case with me and help me close this huge deal.

"Hey, Craig," I asked. "You got a minute?"

"Yeah. What's up?" he said.

"Well," I explained, "I came across an old Aspen ski school instructor who managed to put away five million bucks over his career. He likes some ideas I showed him and wants to do something."

"Yeah, man!" Craig's enthusiasm was so loud the people in the parking lot could hear. "Dude, you are going to max out the quarterly bonus for sure. Congratulations!"

"I hope so," I said. "I didn't want to screw it up so I didn't start any of the paperwork yet. I was hoping you would go out there with me and dust off those old closing skills."

I could see the excitement drain from Craig's face. "That's two hours of driving each way. Why didn't you close it if he liked it?" he asked.

"I just wanted to make sure I was doing the best thing for him," I said. "I panicked."

"Let's see these ideas he liked so much," Craig said. Together he and I went over the ideas I'd written down on a legal pad. We made some adjustments and set up a time to visit my rich ski instructor friend. I could hardly wait. Each day that passed felt like an eternity. Closing a case half that size would take me to the top of leaderboard.

When the day finally came, Craig showed his true mastery. To my surprise he executed every step of the sales cycle just the way I had. When the prospect informed Craig we had gone over this same information in our last meeting, Craig told Butch that he needed to do it again to clarify some of our notes. After the presentation, the prospect reaffirmed that he liked what he heard, but when Craig started filling out the paperwork he stopped him. My heart stopped as well.

"I'm not writing you a check today," he said.

"Sir, I don't understand," Craig said. "Is there something you don't like about what we discussed?"

"No."

Craig pushed. "What do you like most about this new account?" He was trying to help the prospect focus on what he wanted.

"I like the interest I will make," Butch explained. "But I'm not writing you a check and if you try and pressure me with your clever closing crap I'll kick you out of my house." The tension was palpable. I was shocked. He looked at me and said, "Erik, I like you a lot and I want you to come back and see me again. Next time just come by yourself. I wanted to talk more about literature like last time, but we're out of time. I have an appointment with my doctor so we need to finish up here."

Craig and I left feeling totally defeated. Craig had done everything perfectly but had been completely shut down. I had felt so empowered and confident watching him work because I learned there is no special magic to closing a case. The air was let out my balloon when the close fell flat for Craig. I was conflicted discovering I could close anything as well as Craig but sad watching a huge case fall flat before my eyes.

A couple of weeks later I got to visit Butch again. The door was answered by a woman in scrubs who helped me navigate around oxygen lines and medical equipment. I sat next to my friend for a couple of hours. We talked about John Steinbeck and F. Scott Fitzgerald. We had some laughs and he told me it felt great to talk about these things.

"Erik," he said, "a lot of people have been after my money. I just kept it in the bank because I was waiting for someone like you to help me with it. I like you and know that you care about me."

We were being candid and I felt like I wasn't going to have another chance to ask him so I took the leap. "Well," I said, "why did you say no when I brought Craig out?"

His reply will stay with me forever. "Because," he said, "it wasn't you asking to take care of my money."

Three weeks later I showed up at his door with a copy of John Steinbeck's *Tortilla Flat*. His brother answered the door and told me that Butch had passed; I choked back tears. I handed him the book and walked back to my car. As I sat in my car, the irony hit me. The biggest lesson on closing had been given to me by a prospect who became a friend at the end of his life without any business changing hands. He told me I had done my job and all he wanted was for me to close the deal myself. We had walked a path together and he wanted to give me his business. Closing isn't magic; it's the natural conclusion to a sales conversation. If you do everything else right, closing is the easiest part.

Learning on the Last Run

Reflecting on the closing lessons I received from my ski instructor friend, I came to understand that emotion was a deeper and important element to the close. The expert closer I recruited for help followed the same methods but came up wanting. I had made an emotional connection that tipped the decision in my favor and all I had to do was follow through. No special technique, no tricky phrases, just an invitation to do business. It should be noted that most buying decisions are made on emotion and justified by facts.

That was made clear to me when the closing superstar confirmed that Butch liked the opportunity but refused to buy; the emotional connection to close the sale had been lacking.

I had unintentionally built the connection with Butch by focusing on the sales cycle. Our personalities meshed. He was a fan of American literary classics like those of Steinbeck, Hemmingway, and Salinger, and we connected on that level as well. He had married his high school sweetheart as had I. Throughout the course of our time together, business discussions would mingle with personal connections and stories. Emotional connections were made from our introduction, through the needs analysis, and during our collaboration of my presentation. Emotion served as the mortar for the building blocks of our business friendship. People like doing business with people they like; that's emotion.

Oddly enough, most of the emotional connection we established was a result of me saying little but listening a lot. Butch had lived many years and seen many things. I was genuinely interested in his stories. I was following the 70/30 rule of listening—spend 70% of your time listening and only 30% of your time speaking—and I was loving every minute of it. Salespeople often struggle with this rule and frequently reverse it. This usually happens if the emotional connection isn't deep enough and to compensate for situational insecurity, salespeople fill the air with fruitless blubbering, sacrificing the relationship and the sale at the same time. The easy remedy is to work on establishing more of an emotional connection by being genuine and letting the prospect talk. In sales, we want our prospects to be interested in both us as people and our products. It may seem counterintuitive to focus on the client if we are seeking to build interest in our product or service, but the fact remains that the most interesting people tend to be the most interested in others.

Trial Closes

As someone approaches a decision, the tension will naturally rise. Consider a marriage proposal. There is often either excited tension ("I'm nervous even though I'm pretty sure she'll say yes") or unsure tension ("I really hope she says yes"). The difference between the two types of tension is the path taken to get to that point. The path of unsure tension was forged by a personal agenda. In the case of a marriage proposal, there might be family pressure to get married or internal pressure sprouting from the belief that marriage will satisfy personal desire. When the question is asked, there is a selfish hope surrounding the answer. Excited tension is entirely different. That's when you know the answer and the tension is a result of emotional excitement and happiness about moving forward. Couples that experience excited tension have been progressively building their relationship over time. They ask questions about marriage and the meaning of commitment. They spend time learning if the commitment is the right fit for them together. Questions and conversations precede the proposal because nothing should be left to chance in a marriage commitment.

Being a successful closer means building excited tension. We do that by checking in with trial closes. Trial closes are quick questions that verify there is interest building within the sales cycle. "Does that make sense?" or "How would that benefit you?" Checking in during the sales cycle with little questions will build excitement because they engage the prospect. By making sure everyone is on the same page, we can use trial closes to show that we care about them instead of rattling off boring statistics, features, and benefits that they don't care about. Throughout the sales cycle, we can check in to build the relationship and the sale at the same time. Each time we confirm we are on the same page with the prospect, it shows that we care. People feel included when we make sure to collaborate. We can use simple questions like

- Does that make sense?
- You can see why so many people need this, right?
- Tell me your thoughts.
- How would that make a difference?
- How much do you think people usually pay for this?
- How would you use this?

Questions like these allow us to check in at many points during the sales conversation. We verify engagement with questions like "Does that make sense?" without getting off track. We can also deepen our prospect's interest by asking questions that get him or her thinking about how he or she will benefit. Using questions like these allows us to know the answer to the big question before we ask it. Closing will still be tense, but I would rather be excited about it than unsure.

Give Them What They Want

Closing is the natural completion of a successfully executed sales cycle. When a prospect has been ushered through an understanding of their pain and the solution, they should want to give something of value in exchange for the solution. The end of the sales cycle takes on the atmosphere of an offering instead of demanding a decision. A sales professional knows how to casually ease into the terms of the deal by treating the close like the conclusion of a conversation.

Having some prepared methods for closing a sale can be helpful. Finding a comfortable closing method is great; having others from which to draw is professional. Here are a few I like:

- **Assumptive close.** This is one of the most efficient and powerful closes I have used over the years. If the prospect wants to move forward, you can gently transition into handling all the final documents or payment details. When the sales cycle is closely followed, this is one of the most effective ways of completing the sale. "To finalize everything I just need you to start filling out this paperwork" or "What we do now is complete the payment information. I can take cash, check, or any major credit card. Which works best for you?"

- **Triplicate** is a way of offering three options for the prospect to choose from. "Most people I work with like these three options. Which one do you like the most? Which would be most comfortable with the way you budget?" This is a powerful close because it gauges how much value the prospect sees. You can even follow up by asking about the choice if you want to gain further insight on how to improve.

- **Cost per day** is a great way to change the perspective on a big-ticket item. You can divide the cost up over a month, week, or years to enhance the affordability. "Paying a monthly insurance premium at $400 per month will feel a lot better than paying a long-term care facility $400 per day (or more)."

- **Get it before it's gone** is a way of communicating the scarcity of what you offer. Sharing limited-time offers is an act of service and can help people make their decision.

This works when there are quantity limitations, but it can be abused when that's not the case. Using false scarcity to manipulate is plain old lying; don't do it.

- **Feel, felt, found** is a great way of helping someone understand that they aren't alone. "Mr. Prospect, I understand you are feeling a little nervous about paying for my services. I felt the same way when I paid for sales coaching for the first time. What I found was that the coaching process increased my sales income four times over and now I can't thrive without it."

- **Pros and cons list (aka Ben Franklin)** is one more tactic to add to your closing repertoire. Folklore says that Benjamin Franklin would create a pros and cons list when making a difficult decision; this close draws on that decision-making model. Asking the prospect for the cons to the deal gives them a chance to voice their objections. After they finish with the cons, start collaborating on a list of the benefits. If the pros outweigh the cons, the decision to proceed with the sale is deemed wise.

I Didn't See That Coming

No matter how well you did your job throughout the sales cycle, some clients will still not buy. You may have asked the perfect trial close questions, developed needs like a pro, and demonstrated exactly how to solve the problem but when the cost rolls out, the deal still dies. Why? The answer: conditions.

Conditions are nonnegotiable. When the prospect simply doesn't have the money or credit, they won't be able to move forward no matter how much they want to. Timing can also lead to the demise of a sale. An annual budget might be already set or their business income might be seasonal so they won't be able to buy until a different time.

Try to identify nonnegotiable conditions early and don't beat yourself up if they catch you by surprise. No one can close every deal or make every sale. It just doesn't happen. Each surprise we encounter is a learning opportunity and an experience that builds toward mastery.

Stalls are a bit different. Salespeople often run into prospects who can't say no. This sounds exciting but it's actually frustrating because these are usually the prospects who won't say yes either. Not wanting to commit either way, the prospect will stall the sale and keep the salesperson in a holding pattern seemingly forever. They want more information before they make a decision and they always need more time to think. Stallers don't want to hurt anyone's feelings and they loathe confrontation. As a result, a lot of time is wasted.

Handling a suspected staller can be as easy as preparing them when you ease into the close. This kind of preparation saves precious time because it eliminates endless follow-up time with prospects who have no intention to follow through. Many prospects believe that salespeople live to hear "yes" but that's not always the case. Telling them you like hearing "no-go" as much as yes sets the stage for honest feedback. When a staller understands that a "no" is okay, it lets you move on to the next prospect and empowers them to be comfortably honest in declining the offer. You can even tell prospects that you don't accept maybes because you don't have time to follow up, as you have many people who are serious about doing business. It may seem harsh, but being direct and up front with a staller can make all the difference.

Objections will be the easiest hurdle to handle when closing. Always remember that the objections are for the buyer—not the salesperson—to overcome. The best way we can serve our prospects is to help them overcome their objections. When we embrace the mindset of service, we see objections as an opportunity to serve instead of a fine point to haggle over. When we spend time serving our prospects in this way it deepens the relationship we are building with them.

It's Harder to Open

When I was nineteen, I worked at a sporting goods store selling shoes. Every morning the other salespeople and I would watch customers march up to the glass door and yank on the locked door as hard as possible. Looking left to right in disbelief, they would find the sign that displayed the hours and then angrily march back to their car to sit for the remaining fifteen minutes until the store manager would unlock the doors. The best part was watching another shopper make their way to the door after watching the person before them try to open the door in vain. They would jerk the handle, look around in disbelief, and shuffle back to their car like a lemming. It's amazing how much trouble people have with opening and closing doors.

I used to watch customers try to open locked doors and now I talk to salespeople who try to close deals that won't close. Common sense says that locked doors won't open without a key and deals that don't close have something blocking the way. If there is something in the way of a deal closing the best option is to go back through the sales cycle and find out what was left undone. Was pain discovered and developed properly? Did you establish credibility in your introduction? Was there confirmation from the client at the end of your presentation? When you go back and find what's in the way, closing is the easiest part.

Reflecting on our journey through the sales process, closing is just the end of a sales journey. The old perception that success is owned by abusive closers becomes irrelevant when we see how important it is to build relationships throughout the sales journey. Knowing and following a sales process demystifies the "magic" of closing and makes it attainable. If we focus on serving our prospects wholeheartedly by following each step, nothing will prevent us from closing the deal.

CHAPTER 9

Destination – Referrals (AWAKEN)

WHEN YOU LIVE IN THE MOUNTAINS of Colorado with two small sons and are subjected to long, cold winters, wrestling becomes a regular activity. My sons Matthew and Jonathan are nineteen months apart and are practically inseparable. Most mornings, the first one to wake up would pull the other out of bed by the feet, thus beginning the daily brawl. They would put on superhero costumes when they didn't have to go to school and lovingly duke it out with each other. Arial stunts and pillow fights would commence, lasting until lunch. After refueling, they would spend the rest of the afternoon practicing what they had seen in superhero movies or what they had learned in wrestling class.

Early on, Linsey and I decided to get them in a wrestling program so that they would know how to handle themselves safely.

The fights between them were getting pretty vicious and sometimes involved hitting, kicking, and scratching. Knowing that wrestling would help them develop discipline and technique, we found a program through the local high school. Both boys took to wrestling like fish to water. They loved the drills, the matches, and their coach. We didn't foresee how passionate we would become about wrestling as a family. But before we knew it, we were attending wrestling events for eight to ten hours just to see our boys grunt and tussle on the wrestling mats. The whole family would work themselves into a fever pitch as we served as our own cheering section. The boys went on to win medal after medal, making the sport look easy.

A family of six spending ten hours at an athletic event has to find ways to pass the inevitable downtime. Like most families, we would cave to the pressure of our little ones and grant trips to the concession stand. If the kids were good, we would let them buy some licorice. We tried to pack healthy snacks but would always give in to their adorable pleading for pizza slices and Gatorade. Sometimes the matches would start so early they would resist waking up to leave but we would motivate them with the promise of doughnuts awaiting their arrival. It was only a matter of time before we promised the boys a doughnut for first place.

Halfway through the second year of wrestling, the boys started losing matches. We asked them if they still liked wrestling and they reassured us that they did. We didn't understand where the winning edge had gone. We observed them at practice, encouraged them to wrestle at home, and got them the gear they wanted, but nothing seemed to bring the edge back.

During a winter tournament, I noticed Jonathan asking his nana for a dollar about an hour before his match. I followed him and watched him get in line at the concession stand and pull three dollars of his own allowance out of his pocket. Suddenly, I realized where his edge had gone.

I resumed my seat in the bleachers next to Linsey and told her what I had just seen. We sat together and watched Jonathan carefully walk toward us with a paper boat of nachos and a Mountain Dew, smiling from ear to ear. We could do nothing but giggle as we glanced at the huge bag of water, apples, oranges, and whole-wheat fig bars that sat between us untouched.

"Hey, Buddy," Linsey asked. "How did you get the money to buy all of that?"

"I used some of my allowance," Jonathan said. "You said it's my money and I could buy whatever I want."

"Yeah, Bud," I said. "No problem; we were just wondering. Hey, you want to make a deal like we used to last year?" I waited for him to nod before continuing. "If you place first in your weight class we can all go out for ice cream after the match. How does that sound?"

"Seriously?" he asked in disbelief. "What about the diet you and Mom are on?"

"We don't have to eat ice cream," I said. "This will be for you winning first place. You can even have a large if you want."

"I'm in!" he said. "Just remember, you promised."

When it came time for him to wrestle, Jonathan went on to win each match and shut down opponents he had lost to weeks before. Linsey and I chatted after the match while the kids savored their ice cream. We learned that rewards are defined on a case-by-case basis. Our boys were only mildly motivated by the recognition and medals they would be awarded for winning their matches. What made the difference were the simple trips to the concession stand or stops at the ice cream store.

Top-producing salespeople see the prize differently than the salesperson struggling to get by. People who struggle view each potential sale as the prize, while top producers see the sale as the last step along the way to earning the real prize. Struggling salespeople hustle and try to squeeze a prospect to close for a commission. Sales professionals close gently because they are focused on a prize that will make them more money, allow them to work fewer hours, and result in happier clients. Sales professionals see referrals as the real prize.

The Case for Referrals

The impact referrals have on business growth and sales is well covered. The *New York Times* reported that 65% of new business is done by referral. Dale Carnegie Training reports that 91% of customers would give referrals if asked but only 11% of salespeople ever ask. The Nielsen Group reported that prospects are four times more likely to buy when they are referred by someone else. This backs up the Pareto principle in terms of general sales income.

In 1941, Joseph Juran came across the work of Vilfredo Pareto and was able apply his work to business management. In 1896, Mr. Pareto published a paper in which he founded his famous 80/20 rule. In his research he found that 80% of the land in Italy was owned by 20% of the citizens. He even noticed that 20% of his garden peapods produced 80% of the harvested peas. The Pareto principle states that 80% of the effects come from 20% of the causes.

This principle works itself out in the world of sales when we look at the habits of top producers. The top 20% of sales professionals make 80% of the commissions and much of that success comes from being dedicated to asking for referrals. Since referrals are so effective in terms of driving sales, it makes sense to be intentional about asking. And yet only a small segment of salespeople do it. This focus on referrals instead of closing the sale is what gives these successful salespeople the momentum to break through and land in the top 20%.

The twenty-percenter sales territory has some specific dynamics that are helpful to note. When the prize of the sales process is referrals the focus changes from a sales agenda to an extension of service. Focusing on referrals also helps us pay attention to people instead of worrying about our productivity. When we leverage our prospecting time with referrals, we find that we become much more efficient. By being referral- and customer-focused we develop the habit of constantly asking for referrals.

I Can Smell Your Commission Breath

I spend a lot of my time talking to struggling salespeople who want to see big changes fast. Some of them are looking to learn tricky closing techniques, while others are trying to figure out how to churn through more prospects. When you have mouths to feed, a mortgage to pay, and school loans that seem never to go away, your people skills are impacted. Sales is a "people" business and people hate to be pushed. Obligations taunt us to push faster and harder, while sales slow to a stop when people feel they are being forced and coerced. Ironically, sales begin to increase as people experience a slow and easy sales process, but that is a huge challenge with obligations pulling from every direction. There is a subconscious scramble to meet obligations in a business where slow is fast and fast is slow. Being around people long enough confirms that theory. Just try and force someone to do something quickly and you'll find them digging in their heels faster than you can imagine! When we come into a closing situation with an agenda in mind, the prospect can smell the commission on us and will often resist.

When I change my focus to providing value through an amazing experience, I work to earn introductions to my prospect's sphere of influence. The last thing I want to do is come off as greedy or selfish. I want the prospect to have such a good experience that they talk about me the next day to their friends. That's an indication of having a service mindset, and as we've already learned, excellent service makes a huge difference. Approaching with a service mindset gives the salesperson the foundation to form a relationship. And from that relationship comes more sales. People buy from people they like; people refer salespeople they love!

Cover Up! Your Numbers Are Showing

As mentioned before, sales is a numbers game, but making a prospect feel like a number is a sure-fire way to decrease sales. The pressures of life demand that management can lead us to push very hard and increase activity. Having trouble hitting a quota? Call more prospects. Need more money? Book more appointments. The song remains the same, but so do the results. Doing more of an ineffective activity will lead to burn out or, worse, insanity!

It can be hard to adjust your productivity by focusing on referrals instead of sales; it seems counterintuitive. As the referral engine warms up, business might slow down. Sales might dip because prospects will be less pressured to buy something they don't need or want. But you can't give up as the momentum builds. When focused on service, value, and referrals you're acting much like a farmer sowing seeds. Waiting for the harvest might take time, but it will be a great harvest indeed.

When the referral momentum catches up, the big sales numbers that bosses love will begin to roll in naturally. Finally, business will begin to feel effortless and fun. Clients are excited to refer you and time spent with low-return prospecting tends to vanish. With a referral mindset, the managers and bean counters aren't frustrated with your productivity; instead they're frustrated with people who aren't able to make the mindset shift like you did.

Leverage

Archimedes is credited with saying, "Give me a place to stand and a lever and I will move the whole world." Everyone wants to get more work done with less effort. It is really cool to watch a little kid lift a whole car using a tiny car jack. Some of the biggest producers I have encountered mirror that image. These people don't necessarily look like they would be the best of the best but they are because they use sales leverage to get more done. They do seemingly small or insignificant things that create massive results and make getting big commission checks look like child's play.

There are two problems you can have in sales: struggling to find sales and struggling to handle too many. Most people would love to struggle with handling an abundance of business—that comes from having a referral mindset. Referral gathering is a fulcrum between our sales income and our prospecting effort. Moving a fulcrum toward what we are lifting makes the job easier. By putting low importance on referral gathering, we set our pivot point very close to us and must exert a huge amount of force on traditional prospecting methods. When we put our priority on gathering referrals, we move the pivot point closer to the large sales income we want to lift. By doing so, we use less energy to do more work.

Top producers don't talk about themselves as great closers, incredible presenters, or the best prospectors. Rather, they are set apart by the referrals they get. Every day you spend in sales that you don't focus on referrals is a day you spend being average. Make referrals the prize you seek and you'll rise to the top.

It's Not What You Said; It's How You Said It

At one point in my career, I was fortunate enough to work with a man named Paul. Paul was from Jamaica and we worked together in construction management. When I met him, Paul had lived in the United States for over three decades. While in Jamaica he had worked as reporter and had done interviews with politicians and influential people during very turbulent times. Based on Paul's background it was clear that he valued communication so he decided to teach me an unforgettable communication lesson.

Based on my understanding of the Rastafarian religion, I had some assumptions about Jamaicans that Paul decided to leverage against me for a good laugh. Paul liked Bob Marley because of Bob's skill as a musician and his national identity, not for what he smoked. Occasionally I would tease Paul and try to get him to admit to smoking marijuana but he would always laugh and call me a bald-head.[3] Over time I learned that Paul was married and had two boys. One had gone to the United States Naval Academy and played football. Paul's other son was more mysterious and was often calling with money problems. Occasionally he would get calls from his son while at work and he used that to set me up.

---

3 Derogatory Jamaican term used to describe someone who is clean-shaven and politically conservative.

After receiving a call from one of his sons on a beautiful Virginia afternoon, Paul got off the phone rather distraught.

"Is everything okay, Paul?" I asked, seeing that he looked upset.

"Yeah, I guess," he told me. "My son is having money problems again. I get tired of helping him." He feigned a sullen look.

He let a few moments pass and then said, "Did I ever tell you my son is a drug dealer?"

I was shocked. "What?" I said. "And you're okay with that? You're only enabling his behavior by helping him!" I went on and on. "Not only that, but aiding him puts your wife and your livelihood at risk too. You need to stop." I could feel my blood pressure rising as I gave my loving self-righteous sermon.

Letting the tension build a little more, Paul replied, "Why would I not help my son with investment advice? He's looking for the best way to save for my granddaughter's college education. He makes great money working for Pfizer as a pharmaceutical rep and needs to find ways to save money and lower his taxes."

I felt like an idiot as Paul laughed at me for what seemed like an eternity. He explained that my conditioning from American culture tainted many of my interactions. He had noticed these habits as I would interact with him and other colleagues and wanted to help me discover it for myself for the sake of my future success. He used his background as a writer to create the perfect trap and teach me a lesson about communication. I learned that it's not what you say; it's how you say it. Paul wasn't lying when he said that his son was a drug dealer, but it was my assumption that turned it into something insidious.

Most salespeople understand how important it is to ask for referrals; the way they ask is usually the biggest problem. There are many nuances to communication, so with a few adjustments to how we communicate we can get drastically different results. Giving up on gathering referrals because we *think* we are "no good" isn't the way to become successful. Learning a better way to have a referral conversation is the leverage we seek!

Principles Beget Authenticity

"That's great, Erik," you might be saying. "I know referrals are important and focusing on them will transform my sales, but how do I do it? I leave business cards, tell them to call me if they think of someone, and have even asked if they can think of someone on the spot. It doesn't work!"

I understand. I used to feel the same way. I didn't need to know what to say, I just needed to know how to say it. In my search for the perfect script I learned that there is no perfect script. I would try some sales master's wording and get mediocre results. Eventually I realized that problem wasn't the scripting, it was me. I was trying so hard to use someone else's technique that my delivery would come off as inauthentic. I tried writing my own scripts and the result worked a little better. Out of desperation, I sat down and decided to look for common elements in each approach. The result was a principled approach that empowers any salesperson to gather referrals. This new approach was an awakening. It revived my business, eased my prospecting, and saved me time.

AWAKEN

If you are looking for the exact scripting for a referral conversation you won't find it here. Referral conversation principles work much better. These principles build on each other to guide the prospect to thinking about how they can help. People love to help, and if you've done a good job by providing them with good service, they will want to reciprocate and help you! I like to use the pneumonic "AWAKEN" to remember the important elements.

A: Appreciation. When transitioning into the referral conversation it is important to show appreciation. It is easy to be thankful when we make a sale, but gathering referrals from people who don't buy from us is what sets professionals apart from the novices. Leading with appreciation sets the stage for great things to come. We can appreciate the time spent, attention to issues, or the connections made. There is always something we can appreciate, and articulating it matters.

W: Wishful. If I can do it authentically, I love to tell prospects how much I loved working with them. Taking it further, I like to plant a referral seed in their mind. If I want ten referrals from them I give them a hint by saying something like, "I wish I could work with ten people just like you! Our meeting was a real pleasure." By following this principle and giving them a number, they start seeing a group of people in their mind. Following this principle helps connect the isolated sales conversation they had with you into a potential conversation with someone else.

A: Assistance. Asking for help is very powerful. There is an old political adage that says if you want someone to feel indebted to you, ask them for something. People want to help. Helping makes a person feel good. By asking for help you are giving the person you have been helping an opportunity to reciprocate. If they decide to buy, the likelihood they'll want to help is very high. If you have provided value to people who don't buy, there is still a good chance referrals will be made. Don't be afraid to ask for help.

K: Know. Finding out who your prospect knows in the target market is the first part of the referral conversation. Avoid asking them for the names of people who would be interested in your product or service. This part of the conversation should be focused on uncovering people whom you would like to meet. You might be interested in meeting people over sixty-five years old if you are helping people on Social Security. A personal trainer might ask about people who have gym memberships but find it hard to schedule a workout. This phase of the conversation is where your prospect gets warmed up. Your prospect will think of the easy names, so write them down as quick as they come.

E: Envision. The next principle in the referral conversation draws on the prospect's ability to partner with you in growing your business. By asking them who they envision us working with professionally or in the community we let them help us with a different type of referral. From this phase of the conversation we can be introduced to major players in the business community or folks who can amplify our reach. They might give general ideas about groups of people you should meet like chiropractors, CEOs, or councilmen. If they have the idea, chances are they know someone to introduce you to.

N: Niche. At the beginning of the sales cycle and throughout the sales process we learn interesting things along the way. We find out about yoga classes, rotary clubs, church groups, and networking functions that our prospects attend. As we close off the referral conversation, we can begin to ask for introductions to those groups and drive our influence deeper into our target market. When we attend these functions or plug into these groups the prospect or client starts doing the selling for us. It's awesome!

By following these conversation principles anyone can build an effective script for gathering referrals. The principle guides the prospect in a gentle way and helps him or her think of ways to help. Making a commitment to asking for referrals is just another way of serving clients and prospects because if they don't meet you, they might meet the competition who won't give them your incredible level of service.

A Few Referral Tips

Here are some quick tips that make referral gathering a bit more effective. These tips are included because they provide a deeper level of service. They are not manipulative in any way; they are acts of service to make the person feel at ease.

After asking who they know, get your pad of paper and pen ready: This is not a manipulative tactic to make your prospect give you a name. Instead, it allows you to break eye contact so they can think. People don't think well when they're being stared at. A stare down after asking for names feels like an interrogation. Just look at your paper!

Always ask who else: After receiving a name, help the person maintain momentum by asking who else instead of asking for the person's phone number. Continue to ask "Who else?" until they stop giving names; that's the signal to move to the next section of the conversation.

Create the list in layers (names, nuggets, and numbers): It really helps if you focus only on names as you work through the referral conversation. It builds momentum and when I ask for numbers, I tend to end up with fewer referrals. After asking for names, it is great to ask for nuggets, or the little things that help create commonality with the referral. For instance, if your contact is really into golf, that's a good thing to know so you can mention it during your first conversation. It shows that you're paying attention. When you call the person it makes a big difference if you know about their personality or have been told a fun story about how they met your client. The last piece of information you want to get is their cell phone number. You don't want landlines, email addresses, or business phones. By gathering cell numbers, you dramatically increase the likelihood of actually talking to the referral.

The veil of sales is lifted when we start to look at it as a referral and networking business. Instead of looking at prospects as dollar signs to be bludgeoned into a close, we see them as friends connecting us to future business. Business will multiply effortlessly like a car jack lifting a huge vehicle. Envision your expanding network as the prize and the big commission check will follow in due time. By focusing on referrals, you step into the big league of sales, and by asking for them in the right way you will knock it out of the park!

CHAPTER 10

Guide Service – Partnering for Success

UNPACKING ALL THE INFORMATION on this journey can feel daunting. This can happen with anything you care deeply about. I love to cook, but one day I stepped into a restaurant kitchen owned by my in-laws. There were things that looked like the tools I had in my kitchen, but a commercial kitchen is on a whole different level. I felt more overwhelmed than empowered. When feeling overwhelmed the tendency is to shut down and stay in a comfortable place. Nothing good will come from that!

Understanding the science of success will help bring the sales cycle to life. By incorporating the elements of success in exact amounts we can fuel our sales journey in just the right way.

Start with a Recipe

There is a recipe for success that will help us move forward. Bread making has many parallels to success and requires three key ingredients: yeast, water, and flour. Keeping the success recipe simple, we will use three ingredients: inspiration, motivation, and momentum. To generate success in any pursuit it is important to mix the ingredients together in the right order with precision. When they are combined out of order, we can experience dismal results. Obviously, larger batches call for larger amounts of each ingredient, and the ingredients must be proportional. There is a specific amount of each ingredient because there is a science to successful bread making. With the right amount of inspiration mixed with the perfect portion of motivation and some raw momentous action, we end up with a big batch of success. Finding the perfect proportion of the ingredients will take a lifetime for some, while others will discover the recipe seemingly overnight. If you haven't discovered the right amounts for your perfect batch of success, don't worry. With the right recipe you will be on your way in no time!

Inspiration

Jack London wrote, "You can't wait for inspiration. You have to go after it with a club." Mr. London's perspective makes a huge difference for those who find themselves in sales or business as merely a way to make a living. They might look at the potential to make a lot of money or be their own boss and wait for inspiration to club *them* over the head. Meanwhile, time marches on and their personal success never begins. When we find inspiration, we become inspired!

Like the yeast used in bread making, inspiration is living. It needs to be nourished. How do you feed your inspiration? Reading books on sales like you've been doing is a great start. Are you hungry for the pursuit of more sales? Do you wake up at night excited about meeting with interesting people and seeing if you can help them? Are you the type of person who tries to refine your process so you can be more effective? Do you love to learn? Can you see yourself as a successful sales professional using all of the best practices? How do you go after those things?

I have been accused of having a one-track mind when it comes to business, leadership, and sales. I love to talk about those subjects any time and have been known to do so day and night. Linsey has to rein me in at least once a day, but that's a signal to me that I'm maintaining my inspiration. I'm careful to not push people away with my agenda, but I know how important it is to remain focused on my passion. Letting that inspiration wane will affect my motivation.

Motivation

If a batch of bread needs flour, yeast, and water, and inspiration is the living element, the second element we need is a medium in which it all happens. Motivation is the water that gets the process started. Putting yeast and dry flour together isn't enough to make bread come together. The two ingredients will just sit there and all the bread-making potential in the world won't change that. Adding the right amount of water is just as important as having the right amount of motivation.

Too much motivation will water down your success. I have met people who spend all their time and money looking for motivation. The focus on needing motivation impacts their ability to do the work needed to be a success. They end up spending their time searching for motivation, and when they look at the clock, they see it's time to go home for the day! I believe we need motivation daily but it must be in the right proportions. Others tend to marginalize motivation and by doing so they can burn out easily. Task after task they keep their nose to the grindstone and the work becomes dry. It's amazing what a little motivation does for their business success!

Our simple recipe for success parallels bread making with some of the methods we see in the ancient craft. The yeast activates by dissolving into the warm water. I find daily quiet time to mix my inspiration with my motivation to be vitally important in my batch of success. A small amount of time spent letting inspiration and motivation interact isn't wasted time. On the contrary, that quiet time creates some massive growth and momentum.

Momentum

When making bread, the yeast activates with water and is ready to work. The next step is to give the yeast something to work on. Flour is the project that the yeast/water mixture attacks, which yields the dough. When we look at our recipe for success we can see why momentum takes the place of flour. Momentum will be the biggest part of success in the end and when mixed with the right amount of inspiration and motivation it will quadruple the amount of success we'll have.

Momentum is very interesting. It is practical and based in consistency. Momentum is both simple and complex at the same time. The magic of dough expansion and successful momentum are eerily similar. A sack of flour by itself is almost useless but its potential is limitless. The same can be said for momentum. Our simple actions combined with inspiration and motivation create massive results.

By combining these three ingredients together we end up with a result that can benefit others. That's a miracle in itself! Using three common elements in the right proportion and order gives the result exponentially more value than the ingredients alone. In this way we can feed ourselves and others. That's the miracle of success.

Learn the Tools; Use the Tools

After the initial shock of stepping into the kitchen of my in-laws' restaurant wore off, the experience began to take shape and became more exciting. I looked around at grills, ovens, and deep fryers that I had no idea how to operate, but I saw other things that looked familiar. There were refrigerators, knives, and other appliances I recognized; they were just bigger than the ones at home. I could feel the excitement building in me as I recognized the potential to create the amazing cuisine that surrounded me. I was beginning to view this professional kitchen like any other, except on steroids!

As I was standing there taking it all in, my father-in-law, Tom, came in and resumed working on a customer's dish. He hadn't seen me in the kitchen and he wasn't expecting me because I never ventured back to his realm. He was a little startled when he saw me, "Hey, bud! I didn't expect to find you back here! What brought you back?" he asked.

"I just wanted to come back and check things out," I said. "This is really cool back here!"

He beamed from ear to ear. He was very proud of his kitchen and not for the reasons you might think. He loved to prepare delicious meals for people to make them happy. The work he put into each meal was an act of love and service. He took me from the sandwich station to the deep fryers, telling me about all of the delicious things he could do with food. My mouth watered and my mind churned. Tom could tell I was hungry and chomping at the bit to make something. He had inspired and motivated me to start creating something incredible.

"I need to get back to work; I have some orders waiting," he told me. "Make yourself at home and let me know if you need help finding something," he said as he set me loose on the kitchen.

The refrigerators had every raw ingredient I could possibly want, but I didn't know where to start. After Tom had finished up the orders he was working on, he found me looking through the refrigerator in awe.

"Did you find something to eat yet?" he asked.

"I wouldn't even know where to start," I replied.

"Well, what do you feel like having?" he asked. "No, better yet, what do you feel like making?" He asked me out of curiosity. I think he wanted to bond with me a bit, and teaching me how to cook in a commercial kitchen was something he knew well. We spent time brainstorming and he came up with an idea for a breakfast burrito that blew my mind. We scrambled some eggs, chopped up some chicken-fried steak, added a few crispy hash browns, a little cheese, and topped it all off with some sausage gravy. The finished burrito was the best breakfast burrito I had ever had. It tasted amazing but it meant so much more. The experience was full of intimidation, learning, excitement, collaboration, and creative success, all rolled into that burrito. That was one big tasty burrito!

By jumping into the situation with both feet, I set myself up for success. I didn't let unfamiliarity and fear push me out of that kitchen. I was hungry and wouldn't leave without something! There were things I needed to learn even though I had been cooking my whole life. I was going to swallow my pride or go hungry. As uncomfortable as my experience in that restaurant kitchen started out, it ended in success. Tom and I bonded over that experience and we created something amazing.

Every End Is a New Beginning

The first thing I learned to cook was cheese quesadillas. My early childhood was spent in La Selva Beach, in Monterey Bay. In California, poor kids learn to make quesadillas as their first cooking lesson; I fell into that demographic. Working moms teach their kids to make them in the microwave because they don't want the house to burn down while they're working. Making quesadillas was my foundation, and from there I began to build a knowledge base.

My dad had an interesting palate. He taught me how to cook corned beef hash from a can and scramble eggs on the stove. I think he even taught me how to fry spam. It doesn't sound sophisticated, but my cooking skills were growing. Grandma Wilt spent hours in the kitchen and she taught me the art of cookie making while I taught her the art of cookie eating. Later there was Mrs. McKenna, who taught home economics and cooking in high school. I made a giant culinary leap that year. Later came the lessons from my restauranteur father-in-law where I honed confidence and learned to educate my taste buds. The common thread to my culinary evolution was mentorship in one form or another.

It is just as important to have mentors in sales and business. It's been proven that people who have been mentored have a greater chance at success. It's no different in sales and business, and I would venture to say that mentors are more vital to success than in most other industries. Having someone cheering you on from the sidelines makes a huge difference when the days are long and challenging. It's best if they don't have a financial interest in your success because that can put undue pressure on the relationship. The right mentoring relationship will feed your inspiration, motivation, and momentum in a personal way.

Successful people view mentoring in three ways. At times, you will find yourself mentoring those who come along behind you on your path to success. Colleagues will rub shoulders and mentor each other as they collaborate. The most important mentoring relationship is when you are the mentee to someone who can show you the path of success. Taking part in these diverse mentoring relationships is a holistic approach to the concept of mentoring. Mentoring those who come behind you feeds your confidence and promotes your desire to give back. When we collaborate and learn from colleagues, we numb our own ego and swallow our pride while staying current on industry trends. Being mentored by successful people who have forged ahead lets us build on their accomplishments and encourages our own success.

The Journey Begins

Growing up I loved reading J. R. R. Tolkien's novels. There are so many aspects of his writing that appeal to me, but his development of character relationships stands out. Each story highlights multiple relationships, and many of them have mentorship themes woven throughout. The success of every mission depends vitally on the mentorship lessons learned along the way. Just as with Tolkien's stories, we want to set out on our journey but need to find those mentor relationships. Let's examine how to find those relationships that will bring this adventure to life!

In *The Hobbit*, the main character, Bilbo Baggins, meets one of his mentors as part of a job offer. The mysterious wizard, Gandalf, shows up at Mr. Baggins' door and recruits him to fill a vital position for a dangerous mission. With each trial the group faces, Bilbo learns to rely on Gandalf's wisdom while simultaneously learning to trust his own wit. Gandalf spends a great deal of time working to empower his mentee; that is the sign of a great mentor. Sometimes mentor relationships can find us in similar ways. As we take on projects or job offers, we find ourselves being reared by wise sages we would not have met otherwise. Keep your mind open; a mentor may appear as if by magic!

Certain truths about mentoring are made clear in Tolkien's stories. Appointed authority is a logical place from which mentorship should naturally flow. Kings, queens, stewards, and advisors should be trusted sources of advice and counsel but they are often a mixed bag tainted by agenda. The lesson we learn about using those in positions of power as mentors is simple: be careful. Appointed leaders can attain their position through a number of ways: some worked very hard to get there, while others may have manipulated the situation to their advantage. When given the opportunity to be mentored by someone in an appointed position, make sure you ask the right questions. Ask about ethics, values, and principles to ensure that you are aligned.

Exchanging value within a mentor relationship also happens in Tolkien's stories. In the *Lord of the Rings* trilogy, Frodo would not have received the counsel from the rulers along his journey had he not been on a mission to stop a war to end all wars. Everyone would benefit from the peace that Frodo would secure and so they advised and supported him on his journey. Value is exchanged on some level in any type of mentorship, but when there is a clear quid quo pro, the relationship is more intentional and effective.

When the famous leadership expert John Maxwell speaks about learning from incredible mentors, he shares stories of value exchange. He explains that he would spend a good part of his paycheck to sit down with influential leaders to interview them. He goes further by explaining how he would plan family vacations around the towns where these influencers lived. He saw the value in spending time with incredible people who had a lot to offer; those connections pushed his success forward.

As John was paying for these interviews, he was getting a two-fold benefit toward his success. He got great interviews but he was also investing in his own success. If he didn't pay for these important interviews, it would have lowered the overall value. By paying the influencer he interviewed it was clear that he was serious about learning incredibly valuable information that he would definitely put to work. Many bookshelves are filled with great information but it won't be put to work unless the cost is very high. I paid for my college education and I am bound and determined to use the knowledge I paid dearly for!

When my daughter Ella was seven years old she began to get tired of me working so much. She would ask me for attention just to be turned down repeatedly. One winter evening as I was sitting in my chair going over paperwork, Ella came up to me with note. I opened it and found that it was a coupon good for a bathroom cleaning if I would let her sit with me and cuddle through one movie. I put the paperwork down and scooped her up. We cuddled and watched her favorite movie. She loved it and I was just going to let the bathroom cleaning go, but the next day I found her cleaning just like her coupon had promised. I almost told her that she didn't have to but I stopped myself. At that moment, I understood that if I stopped her from cleaning it would cheapen the moment we'd had together. Instead I asked her if she wanted help and she smiled back at me, proud of her sacrifice. "No thanks, Dad," she said. "I got this."

Take time and consider this model of value exchange for your success. When you find the right mentor, there should be a cost involved. John Maxwell paid great influencers so much that it hurt his wallet for an hour of their time. My little Ella made her special time with me a little sweeter by making a sacrifice. As a coach, I pay for professional coaching and because I have skin in the game, I get great results.

Let's Hit the Road

Now that you have your sales road map, ethical sales compass, and an idea of who can help you on your way, you are ready to make some serious progress. The best thing you can do is step out that door and get on with your journey. Knowing there will be both hard times and great times is exciting, but remember to stay in the present and take everything one step at a time. This is a journey and it's meant to be enjoyed!

I hope this book has been a similar experience for you. By making it through these pages we have been embarking on a journey in sales. All the principles we have been considering together are the tools that make for a creative and fun experience that will ultimately benefit your clients. You may be familiar with some of these topics, while others may be challenging and new. Some of the information in this book will be easy to implement right away, while other principles will take practice and time. By taking your time and enjoying the journey, you will be able to use these tools to create something wonderful!

My sincere hope is that our journeys will cross paths one day. We can learn so much from each other; that's what life is all about. This book may or may not have helped you, but I hope that you've learned something. I would love to connect with you either way! Please feel free to email me at e.wilt@prosalesconsulting.com. I wish you the best on your journey ahead.

Be excited. You've got this!

Happy sales.

ERIK WILT has been coaching and training in business for over a decade and has been speaking publicly for 20 years. He has built a successful financial services practice, network marketing organization, construction company, and sales/business consultation practice. Erik has worked with thousands of people all over the U.S. helping them build businesses they can be proud of. He lives in southern Oregon with his wife Linsey and their four amazing children. A coffee and adventure lover, Erik is interested in wine, the outdoors, guitar, and John Steinbeck.

www.ingramcontent.com/pod-product-compliance
Lightning Source LLC
Chambersburg PA
CBHW051807170526
45167CB00005B/1920